A Disciple's Journal
2015

A Guide for Daily Prayer,
Bible Reading, & Discipleship

Steven W. Manskar

DISCIPLESHIP RESOURCES

PO BOX 340003 • NASHVILLE, TN 37203-0003
www.discipleshipresources.org

ISBNs
Print 978-0-88177-728-4
Mobi 978-0-88177-729-1
Epub 978-0-88177-730-7

Cover photo by Joey McNair
Cover design by Joey McNair
Interior by PerfecType

Library of Congress Control Number: 2014936524

Printed in the United States of America

DR 728

O that we may all receive of Christ's fullness,
grace upon grace;
grace to pardon our sins, and subdue our iniquities;
to justify our persons and to sanctify our souls;
and to complete that holy change, that renewal of our hearts,
whereby we may be transformed
into that blessed image wherein thou didst create us.

→ John Wesley ←

Contents

Holy Week

Easter

Season after Pentecost (Ordinary Time)

Advent and Christmas (Year C)

Articles

How to Use *A Disciple's Journal*

A Disciple's Journal is a guide for daily prayer, Bible reading, and discipleship in the Wesleyan tradition. The book is organized to help you maintain a daily practice of Bible reading and prayer. In his sermon "The Means of Grace" John Wesley focused on three essential practices that open hearts and minds to receive and participate in the grace of God:

> *First*, all who desire the grace of God are to wait for it in the way of prayer. This is the express direction of our Lord himself. . . . we are in the plainest manner directed to ask in order to, or as a means of, receiving; to seek in order to find the grace of God, the pearl of great price; and to knock, to continue asking and seeking, if we would enter into his kingdom. . . .

> *Secondly*, all who desire the grace of God are to wait for it in 'searching the Scriptures'. Our Lord's direction with regard to the use of this means is likewise plain and clear. 'Search the Scriptures', . . . 'for they testify of me' (John 5:39). And for this very end did he direct them to search the Scriptures, that they might *believe* in him. . . .

> *Thirdly*, all who desire an increase of the grace of God are to wait for it in partaking of the Lord's Supper. For this also is a direction himself hath given (1 Corinthians 11:23-26). . . . Let all, therefore, who truly desire the grace of God, eat of that bread and drink of that cup.

Wesley encouraged Christians to pray and read Scripture at the beginning and the end of every day. *A Disciple's Journal* is designed to help you habitually open your heart to the power of grace by beginning and ending each day in the presence of the living, Triune God.

Orders for Daily Prayer in the Morning and Night

Pages 14 and 16 contain simple orders for daily prayer in the morning and at night. They are adapted from the Book of Common Prayer. The collects for each day of the week are ancient prayers of the Church. Praying these simple orders of daily prayer with the collects is a way of joining your prayers with Christians around the world and throughout history.

A Disciple's Journal contains two facing pages for each week of the year:

- The left-hand page is a guide for daily Bible reading guided by the Revised Common Lectionary Daily Readings. Two Scripture passages are assigned to each day. The bottom half of the page is divided into four quadrants that correspond to the General Rule of Discipleship (see page 171). Record there what you have done throughout the week in each of the four discipleship categories: compassion, justice, worship, and devotion.

- The right-hand page contains portions of hymns by Charles Wesley and consecutive excerpts from Sermon 48: "Self Denial," by John Wesley unless otherwise indicated. You will also find a prayer for each week based upon the Sunday lessons. These prayers were written for use in the Church by members of the Consultation on Common Texts (www.commontexts.org). They are used by permission.

If you are in a Covenant Discipleship group (see page 173) or other kind of accountability group, bring *A Disciple's Journal* with you to your weekly meeting.

The Daily Lectionary

A lectionary is a systematic way of reading the Bible guided by the Church's liturgical calendar. It helps unite the Church in prayer and worship. Four Scripture lessons are selected for Sunday; two lessons from the Old Testament (one from the historical, wisdom, or prophetic books and a psalm) and two lessons from the New Testament (one from an epistle and one of the gospels).

The Revised Common Lectionary (RCL) is organized as a three-year cycle (A, B, and C). Each year emphasizes one of the Synoptic Gospels (A: Matthew, B: Mark, C: Luke) with significant portions of the Gospel According to John included each year during Lent and Easter. Because the RCL is intended for use in worship, it necessarily neglects significant portions of the Bible. The daily lectionary included with *A Disciple's Journal* fills in the gaps.

The daily lectionary found in *A Disciple's Journal* was developed by the Consultation on Common Texts (www.commontexts.org). It is used here by permission.

You will notice that Sunday appears in the middle of each week of readings. The readings from Thursday to Saturday prepare you to hear the word proclaimed in worship on Sunday. The readings for Monday through Wednesday reflect upon the Word proclaimed in Sunday worship.

The Psalm

Two psalms are appointed for most weeks. The first psalm is to be read with the lessons appointed for Thursday through Saturday. This is the psalm that is also read or sung in worship on Sunday. The second psalm is to be read with the lessons appointed for Monday through Wednesday.

Read the psalm each day to prepare your heart and mind before you read the Scripture lessons. Reading the same psalm for several days is dwelling in God's Word. Allow that Word to fill you. Listen for what God is saying to you, the Church, and the world.

The Hymn

A Charles Wesley hymn is selected for each week. Hymns are an important resource for prayer and theological reflection in the Wesleyan tradition. Like the psalm, it is recommended that the hymn for the week be either said or sung each day. Take time to reflect upon the words and allow them to sink into your heart and mind. Let them become part of you. Memorize them along with the psalm.

Cycle of Intercessions

To help broaden your daily prayer "A Cycle of Intercessions" is provided beginning on page 19. In the Lord's Prayer Jesus instructs us to pray "Your kingdom come, your will be done, on earth as in heaven." The cycle of intercessions is a help that encourages us to pray for the world each day.

A Blessing for the Reader

I pray that *A Disciple's Journal* will be a blessing to you and your small group. If you are not in a small group for mutual accountability and support for growing in holiness of heart and life, I pray that you will find or form one. You will find information about Covenant Discipleship groups on page 173. More information is available online at http://www.gbod.org/covenantdiscipleship.

"Rejoice in the Lord always; again I will say, Rejoice. Let your gentleness be known to everyone. The Lord is near. Do not worry about anything, but in everything by prayer and supplication with thanksgiving let your requests be made known to God. And the peace of God, which surpasses all understanding, will guard your hearts and your minds in Christ Jesus.

"Finally, beloved, whatever is true, whatever is honorable, whatever is just, whatever is pure, whatever is pleasing, whatever is commendable, if there is any excellence and if there is anything worthy of praise, think about these things. Keep on doing the things that you have learned and received and heard and seen . . . and the God of peace be with you" (Philippians 4:4-9).

Rev. Steven W. Manskar, DMin
Director of Wesleyan Leadership
The General Board of Discipleship of
The United Methodist Church
Nashville, Tennessee
smanskar@gbod.org
http://www.gbod.org

O that we could begin this day
in devout meditations,
in joy unspeakable,
and in blessing and praising thee,
who hast given us such good hope
and everlasting consolation.
Lift up our minds
above all these little things below,
which are apt to distract our thoughts;
and keep them above,
till our hearts are fully bent
to seek thee every day,
in the way wherein
Jesus hath gone before us,
though it should be with
the loss of all we here possess.

JOHN WESLEY
A Collection of Prayers for Families

Prayer in the Morning & Night

A Cycle of Intercessions

Prayer in the Morning

CALL TO PRAYER (from Psalm 51)

Open my lips, O Lord,
  and my mouth shall proclaim your praise.
Create in me a clean heart, O God,
  and renew a right spirit within me.
Cast me not away from your presence
  and take not your Holy Spirit from me.
Give me the joy of your saving help again
  and sustain me with your bountiful Spirit.

Glory to the Father, and to the Son, and to the Holy Spirit:
  as it was in the beginning, is now, and will be forever. Amen.

SCRIPTURE *The Psalm and one of the lessons for the day are read.*

SILENCE

HYMN *The hymn for the week may be said or sung;
  the Apostles' Creed (see page 18) may be said.*

PRAYERS FOR OURSELVES AND FOR OTHERS

See A Cycle of Intercessions *on page 19.*

THE LORD'S PRAYER

Our Father in heaven, hallowed be your Name,
  your kingdom come,
  your will be done, on earth as in heaven.
Give us today our daily bread.
Forgive us our sins
  as we forgive those who sin against us.
Save us from the time of trial,
  and deliver us from evil.
For the kingdom, the power,
  and the glory are yours,
  now and for ever. Amen.

THE COLLECT *The collect for the day of the week (see page 15) and/or the
  Wesley Covenant Prayer (see page 18) are said.*

Collects for the Morning

SUNDAY

O God, you make us glad with the weekly remembrance of the glorious resurrection of your Son our Lord: Give us this day such blessing through our worship of you, that the week to come may be spent in your favor; through Jesus Christ our Lord. Amen.

MONDAY *(for Renewal of Life)*

O God, the King eternal, whose light divides the day from the night and turns the shadow of death into the morning: Drive far from us all wrong desires, incline our hearts to keep your law, and guide our feet into the way of peace; that, having done your will with cheerfulness during the day, we may, when night comes, rejoice to give you thanks; through Jesus Christ our Lord. Amen.

TUESDAY *(for Peace)*

O God, the author of peace and lover of concord, to know you is eternal life and to serve you is perfect freedom: Defend us, your humble servants, in all assaults of our enemies; that we, surely trusting in your defense, may not fear the power of any adversaries; through the might of Jesus Christ our Lord. Amen.

WEDNESDAY *(for Grace)*

Lord God, almighty and everlasting Father, you have brought us in safety to this new day: Preserve us with your mighty power, that we may not fall into sin, nor be overcome by adversity; and in all we do, direct us to the fulfilling of your purpose; through Jesus Christ our Lord. Amen.

THURSDAY *(for Guidance)*

Heavenly Father, in you we live and move and have our being: We humbly pray you so to guide and govern us by your Holy Spirit, that in all the cares and occupations of our life we may not forget you, but may remember that we are ever walking in your sight; through Jesus Christ our Lord. Amen.

FRIDAY

Almighty God, whose most dear Son went not up to joy but first he suffered pain, and entered not into glory before he was crucified: Mercifully grant that we, walking in the way of the cross, may find it none other than the way of life and peace; through Jesus Christ your Son our Lord. Amen.

SATURDAY

Almighty God, who after the creation of the world rested from all your works and sanctified a day of rest for all your creatures: Grant that we, putting away all earthly anxieties, may be duly prepared for the service of your sanctuary, and that our rest here upon earth may be a preparation for the eternal rest promised to your people in heaven; through Jesus Christ our Lord. Amen.

Prayer at Night

CALL TO PRAYER

O gracious Light,
> pure brightness of the everliving Father in heaven,

O Jesus Christ, holy and blessed!

Now as we come to the setting of the sun,
> and our eyes behold the evening light,
>> we sing your praises, O God: Father, Son, and Holy Spirit.

You are worthy at all times to be praised by happy voices,
> O Son of God, O Giver of life,
> and to be glorified through all the worlds.

SCRIPTURE *One of the lessons for the day may be read.*

PRAYERS FOR OURSELVES AND FOR OTHERS

See A Cycle of Intercessions *on page 19.*

THE LORD'S PRAYER

Our Father in heaven, hallowed be your Name,
> your kingdom come,
> your will be done, on earth as in heaven.

Give us today our daily bread.

Forgive us our sins
> as we forgive those who sin against us.

Save us from the time of trial,
> and deliver us from evil.

For the kingdom, the power,
> and the glory are yours,
> now and for ever. Amen.

THE COLLECT *The collect for the day of the week (see page 17) and/or the Wesley Covenant Prayer (see page 18) are said.*

Collects for the Night

SUNDAY

Lord God, whose Son, our Savior, Jesus Christ triumphed over the powers of death and prepared for us our place in the new Jerusalem: Grant that we, who have this day given thanks for his resurrection, may praise you in that City of which he is the light, and where he lives and reigns for ever and ever. Amen.

MONDAY

Most holy God, the source of all good desires, all right judgments, and all just works: Give to us, your servants, that peace which the world cannot give, so that our minds may be fixed on the doing of your will, and that we, being delivered from the fear of all enemies, may live in peace and quietness; through the mercies of Christ Jesus our Savior. Amen.

TUESDAY

Be our light in the darkness, O Lord, and in your great mercy defend us from all perils and dangers of this night; for the love of your Son, our Savior Jesus Christ. Amen.

WEDNESDAY

O God, the life of all who live, the light of the faithful, the strength of those who labor, and the repose of the dead: We thank you for the blessings of the day that is past, and humbly ask for your protection through the coming night. Bring us in safety to the morning hours; through him who died and rose again for us, your Son our Savior Jesus Christ. Amen.

THURSDAY

Lord Jesus, stay with us, for evening is at hand and the day is past; be our companion in the way, kindle our hearts, and awaken hope, that we may know you as you are revealed in Scripture and the breaking of bread. Grant this for the sake of your love. Amen.

FRIDAY

Lord Jesus Christ, by your death you took away the sting of death: Grant to us your servants so to follow in faith where you have led the way, that we may at length fall asleep peacefully in you and wake up in your likeness; for your tender mercies' sake. Amen.

SATURDAY

O God, the source of eternal light: Shed forth your unending day upon us who watch for you, that our lips may praise you, our lives may bless you, and our worship tomorrow give you glory; through Jesus Christ our Lord. Amen.

The Apostles' Creed

I believe in God, the Father almighty,
    creator of heaven and earth;
I believe in Jesus Christ his only Son our Lord;
        who was conceived by the power of the Holy Spirit,
        and born of the Virgin Mary,
        He suffered under Pontius Pilate,
            was crucified, died, and was buried.
        He descended to the dead.
        On the third day he rose again.
        He ascended into heaven,
            and is seated at the right hand of the Father.
        He will come again to judge the living and the dead.
I believe in the Holy Spirit,
    the holy catholic church,
    the communion of saints,
    the forgiveness of sins,
    the resurrection of the body,
    and the life everlasting. Amen.

Wesley Covenant Prayer

I am no longer my own, but thine.
Put me to what thou wilt, rank me with whom thou wilt.
Put me to doing, put me to suffering.
Let me be employed by thee or laid aside for thee,
    exalted for thee or brought low for thee.
Let me be full, let me be empty.
Let me have all things, let me have nothing.
I freely and heartily yield all things
    to thy pleasure and disposal.
And now, O glorious and blessed God,
    Father, Son, and Holy Spirit,
    thou art mine, and I am thine. So be it.
And the covenant which I have made on earth,
    let it be ratified in heaven. Amen.

A Cycle of Intercessions

Prayers may include the following concerns if it is desired to pray for different topics through the week and the seasons.

Every Day

- In the morning: the day and its tasks; the world and its needs; the Church and her life
- In the evening: peace; individuals and their needs

In Ordinary Time

Sunday

- The universal Church
- Bishops, annual conferences, central conferences, and all who lead the Church
- The leaders of the nations
- The natural world and the resources of the earth
- All who are in any kind of need

Monday

- The media and the arts
- Farming and fishing
- Commerce and industry
- Those whose work is unfulfilling, stressful, or fraught with danger
- All who are unemployed

Tuesday

- All who are sick in body, mind, or spirit
- Those in the midst of famine or disaster
- Victims of abuse and violence, intolerance and prejudice
- Those who are bereaved
- All who work in the medical and healing professions

Wednesday

- The social services
- All who work in the criminal justice system
- Victims and perpetrators of crime
- The work of aid agencies throughout the world
- Those living in poverty or under oppression

Thursday

- Local government and community leaders
- All who provide local services
- Those who work with young or elderly people
- Schools, colleges, and universities
- Emergency and rescue organizations

Friday

- The president of the United States, members of Congress, and the armed forces
- Peace and justice in the world
- Those who work for reconciliation
- All whose lives are devastated by war and civil strife
- Prisoners, refugees, and homeless people

Saturday

- Our homes, families, friends, and all whom we love
- Those whose time is spent caring for others
- Those who are close to death
- Those who have lost hope
- The worship of the Church

In Seasonal Time

Advent

- The Church, that she may be ready for the coming of Christ
- The leaders of the Church
- The nations, that they may be subject to the rule of God
- Those who are working for justice in the world
- The broken, that they may find God's healing

Christmas

- The Church, especially in places of conflict
- The Holy Land, for peace with justice, and reconciliation
- Refugees and asylum seekers
- Homeless people
- Families with young children

Epiphany

- The unity of the Church
- The peace of the world

- The revelation of Christ to those from whom his glory is hidden
- All who travel

Lent

- Those preparing for baptism and confirmation
- Those serving through leadership
- Those looking for forgiveness
- Those misled by the false gods of this present age
- All who are hungry

Holy Week

- The persecuted Church
- The oppressed peoples of the world
- All who are lonely
- All who are near to death
- All who are facing loss

Easter

- The people of God, that they may proclaim the risen Lord
- God's creation, that the peoples of the earth may meet their responsibility to care
- Those in despair and darkness, that they may find the hope and light of Christ
- Those in fear of death, that they may find faith through the resurrection
- Prisoners and captives

Ascension until Pentecost

- Those who wait on God, that they may find renewal
- The earth, for productivity and for fruitful harvests
- All who are struggling with broken relationships

All Saints until Advent

- The saints on earth, that they may live as citizens of heaven
- All people, that they may hear and believe the word of God
- All who fear the winter months
- All political leaders, that they may imitate the righteous rule of Christ
- All who grieve or wait with the dying

O that we might heartily surrender our wills to thine;
that we may unchangeably cleave unto it,
with the greatest and most entire affection to all thy commands.
O that there may abide for ever in us
such a strong and powerful sense of thy mighty love
towards us in Christ Jesus,
as may constrain us freely and willingly to please thee,
in the constant exercise of righteousness and mercy,
temperance and charity, meekness and patience,
truth and fidelity;
together with such an humble, contented, and peaceable spirit,
as may adorn the religion of our Lord and Master.
Yea, let it ever be the joy of our hearts to be righteous,
as thou art righteous;
to be merciful, as thou, our heavenly Father, art merciful;
to be holy, as thou who hast called us art holy,
to be endued with thy divine wisdom,
and to resemble thee in faithfulness and truth.
O that the example of our blessed Savior
may be always dear unto us,
that we may cheerfully follow him in every holy temper,
and delight to do thy will, O God.
Let these desires, which thou hast given us,
never die or languish in our hearts,
but be kept always alive, always in their vigor and force,
by the perpetual inspirations of the Holy Ghost.

JOHN WESLEY
A Collection of Prayers for Families

Journal

Help us to build each other up,
Our little stock improve;
Increase our faith, confirm our hope,
And perfect us in love.

CHARLES WESLEY

The Christian Year

The Christian Year organizes the worship of the Church to help Christians rehearse the life and ministry of Jesus and to disciple others in his way. The Christian Year combines evangelism, teaching, worship, the formation of disciples and mission, and helps the Church keep all of these vital elements of its life and ministry constantly before it.

Advent

Ultimate Salvation

The Christian Year begins with the end in mind. Advent focuses primarily on the fulfillment of all things in Jesus Christ. It begins by reminding us of the Second Advent (coming) of Christ, the final judgment, the resurrection of the dead, and new creation. We then spend two weeks with the prophet known as John the Baptizer whose ministry and preaching about the judgment and end of this current age laid the groundwork for the teaching and ministry of Jesus. The final Sunday of Advent brings us to events leading up to the birth of Jesus.

Advent starts to work in us like a funnel. The purpose of a funnel is to concentrate everything that can flow into it into a smaller outlet so everything can fit into a smaller space. Advent takes in all of history from the "top" and concentrates it and all its meanings on one person, Jesus Christ. It takes in all time, past and future, and moving backward in time, leads us to the incarnation of God in Jesus Christ. It takes in the whole cosmos and its complete renewal and leads us to the confusing and messy, which is to say, very human circumstances surrounding the birth of Jesus. It challenges us to take in the infinitely vast and incomprehensible and to see, hear, and feel how all of it flows out of the son of Mary.

But the aim of Advent is not to fill our heads with grand ideas. Advent, like the age to come it proclaims again and again, is intended to do nothing less than call us to repent and live the good news that God's kingdom, which will complete all that Advent describes, has drawn near.

This is why Advent, like Lent, was also designed as a season for preparing persons for baptism.

As you read and pray daily this Advent, allow the funnel to do its work in you. But more than this, expect the Spirit's refilling, even now, to make all things new in you.

Rev. Taylor Burton-Edwards

November 30: First Sunday of Advent

Preparation for Sunday
Psalm 80:1-7, 17-19

Thursday
Zechariah 13:1-9
Revelation 14:6-13

Friday
Zechariah 14:1-9
1 Thessalonians 4:1-18

Saturday
Micah 2:1-13
Matthew 24:15-31

Sunday
Isaiah 64:1-9
Psalm 80:1-7, 17-19
1 Corinthians 1:3-9
Mark 13:24-37

Reflection on Sunday
Psalm 79

Monday
Micah 4:1-5
Revelation 15:1-8

Tuesday
Micah 4:6-13
Revelation 18:1-10

Wednesday
Micah 5:1-5a
Luke 21:34-38

The General Rule of Discipleship
*To witness to Jesus Christ in the world and to follow his teachings
through acts of compassion, justice, worship, and devotion under the guidance of the Holy Spirit.*

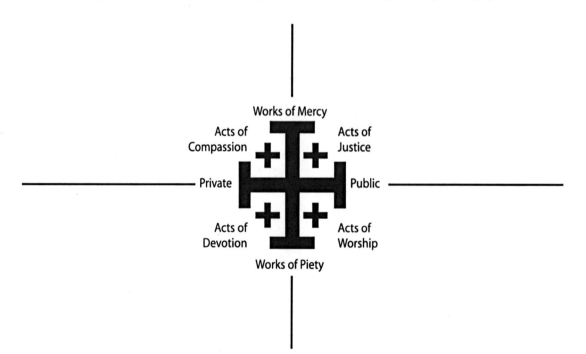

A Word from John Wesley

The person by whom God will judge the world, is his only-begotten Son, whose "goings forth are from everlasting;" "who is God over all, blessed for ever." Unto Him, being "the outbeaming of his Father's glory, the express image of his person" (Heb. 1:3), the Father "hath committed all judgment, because he is the Son of Man" (John 5:22, 27); because, though he was" in the form of God, and thought it not robbery to be equal with God, yet he emptied himself, taking upon him the form of a servant, being made in the likeness of men" (Phil. 2:6, 7); yea, because, "being found in fashion as a man, he humbled himself" yet farther, "becoming obedient unto death, even the death of the cross. Wherefore God hath highly exalted him," even in his human nature, and "ordained him," as man, to try the children of men, "to be the Judge both of the quick and dead;" both of those who shall be found alive at his coming, and of those who were before gathered to their fathers.

(Sermon 15: "The Great Assize," §II.1)

A Hymn from Charles Wesley

Hearken to the solemn voice,
The awful midnight cry!
Waiting souls, rejoice, rejoice,
And see the bridegroom nigh!
Lo! he comes to keep his word;
Light and joy his looks impart;
Go ye forth to meet your Lord,
And meet him in your heart.

Wait we all in patient hope
Till Christ the Judge shall come;
We shall soon be all caught up
To meet the general doom;
In an hour to us unknown,
As a thief in deepest night,
Christ shall suddenly come down
With all his saints in light.

Happy he whom Christ shall find
Watching to see him come;
Him the Judge of all mankind
Shall bear triumphant home;
Who can answer to his word?
Which of you dares meet his day?
'Rise, and come to Judgment'—Lord,
We rise, and come away.

(*Collection*-1781, #53:1, 4, & 5)*

Prayers, Comments, & Questions

God of justice and peace, from the heavens you rain down mercy and kindness, that all on earth may stand in awe and wonder before your marvelous deeds. Raise our heads in expectation, that we may yearn for the coming day of the Lord and stand without blame before your Son, Jesus Christ, who lives and reigns for ever and ever. Amen.

*Hymns labeled *Collection-1781* are from *A Collection of Hymns for the Use of The People Called Methodists* published by John Wesley in 1781.

December 7: Second Sunday of Advent

Preparation for Sunday
Psalm 85:1-2, 8-13

Thursday
Hosea 6:1-6
1 Thessalonians 1:2-10

Friday
Jeremiah 1:4-10
Acts 11:19-26

Saturday
Ezekiel 36:24-28
Mark 11:27-33

Sunday
Isaiah 40:1-11
Psalm 85:1-2, 8-13
2 Peter 3:8-15a
Mark 1:1-8

Reflection on Sunday
Psalm 27

Monday
Isaiah 26:7-15
Acts 2:37-42

Tuesday
Isaiah 4:2-6
Acts 11:1-18

Wednesday
Malachi 2:10–3:1
Luke 1:5-17

The General Rule of Discipleship

To witness to Jesus Christ in the world and to follow his teachings
through acts of compassion, justice, worship, and devotion under the guidance of the Holy Spirit.

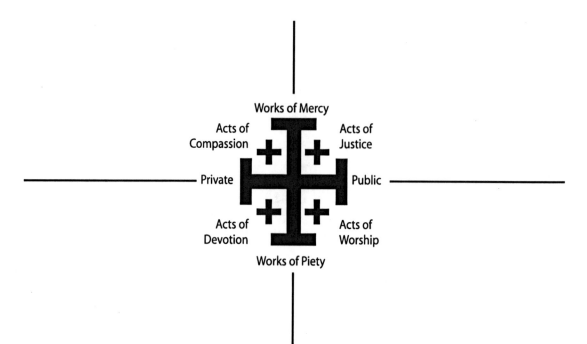

A Word from John Wesley

"Then the King will say to them upon his right hand, Come, ye blessed of my Father. For I was hungry, and ye gave me meat; thirsty, and ye gave me drink: I was a stranger, and ye took me in; naked, and ye clothed me." In like manner, all the good they did upon earth will be recited before men and angels; whatsoever they had done, either in word or deed, in the name, or for the sake, of the Lord Jesus. All their good desires, intentions, thoughts, all their holy dispositions, will also be then remembered; and it will appear, that though they were unknown or forgotten among men, yet God noted them in his book. All their sufferings likewise for the name of Jesus, and for the testimony of a good conscience, will be displayed unto their praise from the righteous Judge, their honour before saints and angels, and the increase of that "far more exceeding and eternal weight of glory."

(Sermon 15: "The Great Assize," §II.8)

A Hymn from Charles Wesley

He comes! he comes! the Judge severe!
The seventh trumpet speaks him near;
His light'nings flash, his thunders roll;
How welcome to the faithful soul!

From heaven angelic voices sound,
See the almighty Jesus crowned!
Girt with omnipotence and grace,
And glory decks the Saviour's face!

Descending on his azure throne,
He claims the kingdoms for his own;
The kingdoms all obey his word,
And hail him their triumphant Lord!

Shout all the people of the sky,
And all the saints of the Most High;
Our Lord, who now his right obtains,
For ever and for ever reigns.

(*Collection*-1781, #55)

Prayers, Comments & Questions

God of timeless grace, you fill us with joyful expectation. Make us ready for the message that prepares the way, that with uprightness of heart and holy joy we may eagerly await the kingdom of your Son, Jesus Christ, who reigns with you and the Holy Spirit, now and for ever. Amen.

December 14: Third Sunday of Advent

Preparation for Sunday
Psalm 126

Thursday
Habakkuk 2:1-5
Philippians 3:7-11

Friday
Habakkuk 3:2-6
Philippians 3:12-16

Saturday
Habakkuk 3:13-19
Matthew 21:28-32

Sunday
Isaiah 61:1-4, 8-11
Psalm 126 *or*
    Luke 1:46b-55
1 Thessalonians 5:16-24
John 1:6-8, 19-28

Reflection on Sunday
Psalm 125

Monday
1 Kings 18:1-18
Ephesians 6:10-17

Tuesday
2 Kings 2:9-22
Acts 3:17–4:4

Wednesday
Malachi 3:16–4:6
Mark 9:9-13

The General Rule of Discipleship
To witness to Jesus Christ in the world and to follow his teachings
through acts of compassion, justice, worship, and devotion under the guidance of the Holy Spirit.

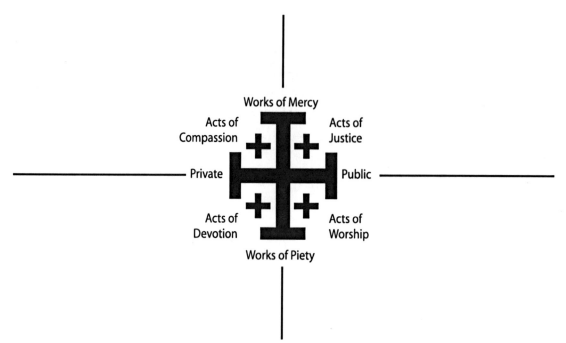

A Word from John Wesley

O make proof of his mercy, rather than his justice; of his love, rather than the thunder of his power! He is not far from every one of us; and he is now come, not to condemn, but to save the world. He standeth in the midst! Sinner, doth he not now, even now, knock at the door of thy heart? O that thou mayest know, at least in this thy day, the things that belong unto thy peace! O that ye may now give yourselves to Him who gave himself for you, in humble faith, in holy, active, patient love! So shall ye rejoice with exceeding joy in his day, when he cometh in the clouds of heaven.

(Sermon 15: "The Great Assize," §IV.5)

A Hymn from Charles Wesley

Ye virgin souls arise,
With all the dead awake.
Unto salvation wise,
Oil in your vessels take:
Upstarting at the midnight cry,
Behold the heavenly bridegroom nigh.

He comes, he comes to call
The nations to his bar,
And raise to glory all
Who fit for glory are;
Made ready for your full reward,
Go forth with joy to meet your Lord.

Then let us wait to hear
The trumpet's welcome sound,
To see our Lord appear,
Watching let us be found;
When Jesus doth the heavens bow,
Be found—as, Lord, thou find'st us now!

(*Collection*-1781, #64:1, 2, & 6)

Prayers, Comments & Questions

God of hope, you call us home from the exile of selfish oppression to the freedom of justice, the balm of healing, and the joy of sharing. Make us strong to join you in your holy work, as friends of strangers and victims, companions of those whom others shun, and as the happiness of those whose hearts are broken. We make our prayer through Jesus Christ our Lord. Amen.

December 21: Fourth Sunday of Advent

Preparation for Sunday
Psalm 89:1-4, 19-26

Thursday
2 Samuel 6:1-11
Hebrews 1:1-4

Friday
2 Samuel 6:12-19
Hebrews 1:5-14

Saturday
Judges 13:2-24
John 7:40-52

Sunday
2 Samuel 7:1-11, 16
Luke 1:46b-55 *or*
    Psalm 89:1-4, 19-26
Romans 16:25-27
Luke 1:26-38

Reflection on Sunday
Psalm 96

Monday
Zephaniah 3:8-13
Romans 10:5-13

Tuesday
Zephaniah 3:14-20
Romans 13:11-14

Wednesday, *Christmas Eve*
Ecclesiastes 3:1-8
James 1:17-18

The General Rule of Discipleship
*To witness to Jesus Christ in the world and to follow his teachings
through acts of compassion, justice, worship, and devotion under the guidance of the Holy Spirit.*

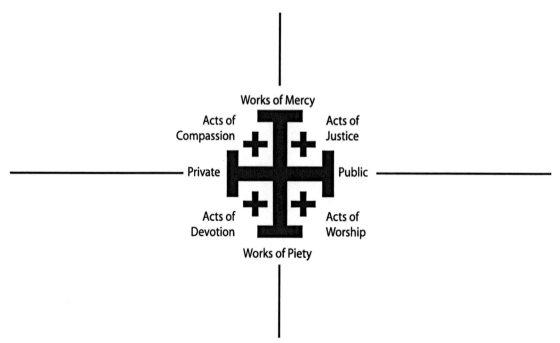

A Word from John Wesley

. . . (T)his was the one end of our redemption; of all our blessed Lord did and suffered for us; of his incarnation, his life, his death? All these miracles of love were wrought with no other view than to restore us to health and freedom. Thus himself testifies of the end of his coming into the world: "The Spirit of the Lord is upon me; he hath sent me to heal the brokenhearted, to preach deliverance to the captives"; or, as the prophet expresses it, "to preach good tidings to the meek, to bind up the brokenhearted, to proclaim liberty to the captives, and the opening of the prison to them that are bound". For this only he lived, that he might heal every disease, every spiritual sickness of our nature . . .

Sermon 146: "The One Thing Needful," §II.3

A Hymn from Charles Wesley

Father our hearts we lift,
Up to thy gracious throne,
And bless thee for the precious gift,
Of thine incarnate Son:
The gift unspeakable,
We thankfully receive,
And to the world thy goodness tell,
And to thy glory live.

Jesus the holy child,
Doth by his birth declare,
That God and man are reconciled,
And one in him we are:
Salvation through his name
To all mankind is given,
And loud his infant cries proclaim,
A peace 'twixt earth and heaven.

(*Hymns for the Nativity of Our Lord*-1745, #9:1 & 2)

Prayers, Comments & Questions

O God of Elizabeth and Mary, you visited your servants with news of the world's redemption in the coming of the Savior. Make our hearts leap with joy, and fill our mouths with songs of praise, that we may announce glad tidings of peace, and welcome the Christ in our midst. Amen.

Christmas Season

The Aftermath of Incarnation

After Advent has "funneled" the cosmos into the cradle, Christmas Season opens up for us the global effects of the Word made flesh. Christmas Season is twelve days, starting with Christmas Eve, during which the Church can begin to unpack and wonder anew at all the birth itself began to unleash then and continues to set loose now.

The readings for Christmas Season are full of violence and danger, and bookended around these stories, blessing. We begin (Christmas Eve and Epiphany) with the joyous announcement of angels to shepherds and Magi interpreting the stars. Between and around them we encounter the violence of Herod, hear of the genocidal deaths of thousands of male infants, and follow the family of Jesus on a desperate journey into Egypt, not unlike the journey of Jacob's family. We remember the first Christian martyr, the deacon Stephen. We hear of Jesus' circumcision and are reminded of the poverty of his family when we learn the sacrificial animals they could purchase for the rite of purification for Mary were those reserved for the poor.

All of these stories, and others we recount from the Bible, are there to keep us mindful that the kingdoms of this world do not welcome the coming of the kingdom of God but violently resist it. They bear daily witness to the reading from the Gospel of John for Christmas Day: "He came to his own, and his own did not receive him." This is why we take the time to prepare persons and sponsors for baptism and discipleship. The world as we know it is not set up to receive our witness to Jesus. Indeed, it sets up myriad ways to put our witness to a violent and, from its angle at least, a shameful end.

But in and through all of these stories of opposition, we also remember the earlier words of our reading from Christmas Day: "The light shines in the darkness, and the darkness did not overcome it." And we are called to rehearse through these days, especially if we are accompanying candidates and sponsors toward baptism, that what we are given in Jesus is nothing less than to become, like him, children of God born not of our own striving, but by water and the Holy Spirit.

Rev. Taylor Burton-Edwards

December 28: First Sunday after Christmas

Preparation for Sunday
Psalm 148

Thursday, *Christmas Day*
Isaiah 52:7-10; Psalm 98
Hebrews 1:1-12
John 1:1-14

Friday
Jeremiah 26:1-9, 12-15
Acts 6:8-15; 7:51-60

Saturday
Exodus 33:18-23
1 John 1:1-9

Sunday
Isaiah 61:10–62:3
Psalm 148
Galatians 4:4-7
Luke 2:22-40

Reflection on Sunday
Psalm 20

Monday
Isaiah 49:5-15
Matthew 12:46-50

Tuesday
Proverbs 9:1-12
2 Peter 3:8-13

Wednesday
1 Kings 3:5-14
John 8:12-19

The General Rule of Discipleship
To witness to Jesus Christ in the world and to follow his teachings
through acts of compassion, justice, worship, and devotion under the guidance of the Holy Spirit.

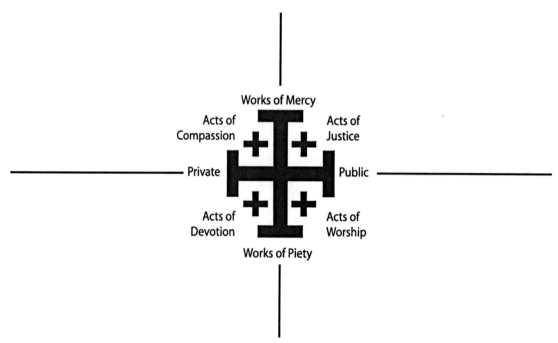

A Word from John Wesley

When he was incarnate and became man, he recapitulated in himself all generations of mankind, making himself the centre of our salvation, that what we lost in Adam, even the image and likeness of God, we might receive in Christ Jesus. By the Holy Ghost coming upon Mary, and the power of the highest over-shadowing her, the incarnation of Christ was wrought, and a new birth, whereby man should be born of God, was shown; that as by our first birth we did inherit death, so by this birth we might inherit life.

Sermon 141: "On the Holy Spirit," §II

A Hymn from Charles Wesley

Glory be to God on high,
And Peace on Earth descend;
God comes down. He bows the sky.
He shows himself our Friend!
God the Invisible appears,
God the Blest, the Great I Am
Sojourns in this vale of tears,
And Jesus is his Name.

See the Eternal Son of God
A mortal Son of Man,
Dwelling in an Earthly clod
Whom heaven cannot contain!
Stand amazed ye heavens at this!
See the Lord of Earth and skies
Humbled to the dust He is,
And in a Manger lives.

(*Hymns for the Nativity of Our Lord*-1745, #4:1 & 3)

Prayers, Comments & Questions

O Holy One, heavenly angels spoke to earthly shepherds and eternity entered time in the child of Bethlehem. Through the telling of the Christmas story, let our temporal lives be caught up in the eternal in that same child, that we might join shepherds and all the heavenly host in praising the coming of Jesus Christ, our Savior. Amen.

January 4: Second Sunday after Christmas

Preparation for Sunday
Psalm 8

Thursday
Holy Name of Jesus
Numbers 6:22-27; Psalm 8
Philippians 2:5-11
Luke 2:15-21

Friday
Proverbs 1:1-7
James 3:13-18

Saturday
Proverbs 1:20-33
James 4:1-10

Sunday
Jeremiah 31:7-14
Psalm 147:12-20
Ephesians 1:3-14
John 1:1-18

Days around Epiphany
Psalm 110

Monday
Proverbs 22:1-9
Luke 6:27-31

Tuesday, *Epiphany of the Lord*
Isaiah 60:1-6
Psalm 72:1-7, 10-14
Ephesians 3:1-12
Matthew 2:1-12

Wednesday
Exodus 1:22–2:10
Hebrews 11:23-26

The General Rule of Discipleship
*To witness to Jesus Christ in the world and to follow his teachings
through acts of compassion, justice, worship, and devotion under the guidance of the Holy Spirit.*

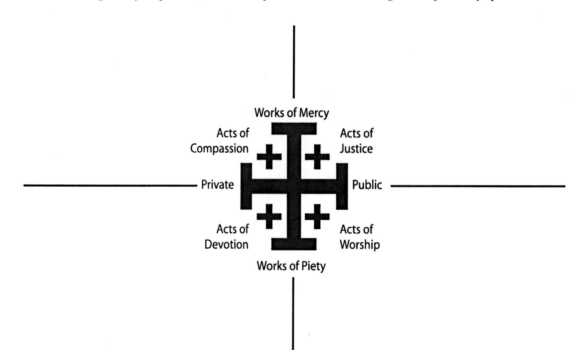

A Word from John Wesley

. . . (I)t is impossible for any that have it, to conceal the religion of Jesus Christ. This our Lord makes plain beyond all contradiction, by a two-fold comparison: "Ye are the light of the world: A city set upon a hill cannot be hid." Ye Christians are "the light of the world," with regard both to your tempers and actions. Your holiness makes you as conspicuous as the sun in the midst of heaven. As ye cannot go out of the world, so neither can ye stay in it without appearing to all mankind. . . . Love cannot be hid any more than light; and least of all, when it shines forth in action, when ye exercise yourselves in the labour of love, in beneficence of every kind. As well may men think to hide a city, as to hide a Christian; yea, as well may they conceal a city set upon a hill, as a holy, zealous, active lover of God and man.

Sermon 24: "Upon Our Lord's Sermon on the Mount IV, §II.2

A Hymn from Charles Wesley

Where is the holy heavenborn Child,
Heir of the everlasting Throne,
Who Heaven and Earth hath reconciled,
And God and man rejoined in one?

Shall we of earthly kings enquire,
To courts or palaces repair?
The nation's Hope, the world's Desire,
Alas! we cannot find Him there.

Shall learning show the sinner's Friend.
Or scribes a sight of Christ afford?
Us to his natal place they send,
But never go to see their Lord.

We search the outward Church in vain,
They cannot Him we seek declare,
They have not found the Son of Man,
Or known the sacred Name they bear.

Then let us turn no more aside,
But use the Light Himself imparts,
His Spirit is our surest Guide,
His Spirit glimmering in our hearts.

(*Hymns for the Nativity of Our Lord*-1745, #17: 1–5)

Prayers, Comments & Questions

God of glory, your splendor shines from a manger in Bethlehem, where the Light of the world is humbly born into the darkness of human night. Open our eyes to Christ's presence in the shadows of our world, so that we, like him, may become beacons of your justice, and defenders of all for whom there is no room. Amen.

The Season after Epiphany

Beginnings of Salvation and Ministry

The Season after Epiphany is bookended by two celebrations: Baptism of the Lord, on the first Sunday after Epiphany and the Transfiguration of Jesus on the last Sunday, prior to Ash Wednesday. The sweep of these Sundays and the days between them prefigures the sweep of the Christian life, from justification and initiation (Baptism of the Lord) to entire sanctification (Transfiguration). While this season is of varying length because of the varying dates of Easter, and so the varying starting time for Ash Wednesday, its purpose is always to help the congregation "get ready to get ready." That is, this is the "introductory course," if you will, to the more intensive preparation for baptism and new commitments in discipleship Lent is designed to help the church undertake.

On the Sundays between Baptism of the Lord and Transfiguration, the Sunday readings from the Old Testament are chosen to correspond with the gospel readings, which cover the early ministry of Jesus. The Epistle readings are not chosen to correspond with the other two, but rather to present a "semi-continuous" reading that will be picked up again during the Season after Pentecost. Though the Epistle readings do not directly connect to the gospel, they do still lay out basics of Christian life. This gives individuals reading daily and worship leaders planning for weekly celebration two distinct paths they may follow during this season, either of which may contribute to its purpose. As you undertake your readings through these weeks, you may wish to coordinate the attention you give to the daily readings based on the focus your worship leaders have chosen for Lord's Day worship to gain the maximum benefit from the correlation of the two.

Rev. Taylor Burton-Edwards

January 11: Baptism of the Lord

Preparation for Sunday
Psalm 29

Thursday
1 Samuel 3:1-21
Acts 9:10-19a

Friday
1 Samuel 16:1-13
1 Timothy 4:11-16

Saturday
1 Kings 2:1-4, 10-12
Luke 5:1-11

Sunday
Genesis 1:1-5
Psalm 29
Acts 19:1-7
Mark 1:4-11

Reflection on Sunday
Psalm 69:1-5, 30-36

Monday
Genesis 17:1-13
Romans 4:1-12

Tuesday
Exodus 30:22-38
Acts 22:2-16

Wednesday
Isaiah 41:14-20
John 1:29-34

The General Rule of Discipleship
To witness to Jesus Christ in the world and to follow his teachings
through acts of compassion, justice, worship, and devotion under the guidance of the Holy Spirit.

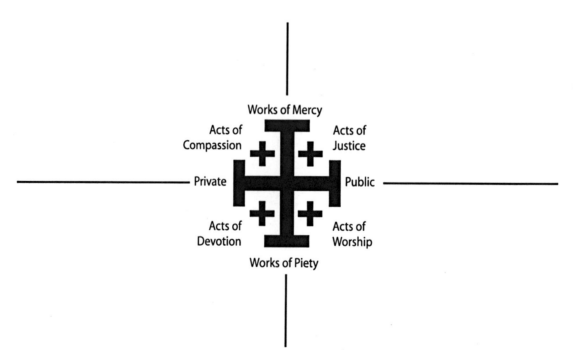

A Word from John Wesley

Sermon 48: "Self Denial"
Luke 9:23

1. It has been frequently imagined, that the direction here given related chiefly, if not wholly, to the Apostles; at least, to the Christians of the first ages, or those in a state of persecution. But this is a grievous mistake: For although our blessed Lord is here directing his discourse more immediately to his Apostles, and those other disciples who attended him in the days of his flesh; yet, in them he speaks to us, and to all mankind, without any exception or limitation.

A Hymn from Charles Wesley

Come, let us use the grace divine,
And all, with one accord,
In a perpetual covenant join
Ourselves to Christ the Lord.

Give up ourselves, through Jesu's power,
His name to glorify;
And promise, in this sacred hour,
For God to live and die.

The covenant we this moment make
Be ever kept in mind:
We will no more our God forsake,
Or cast his words behind.

To each the covenant blood apply,
Which takes our sins away;
And register our names on high,
And keep us to that day.

(*Short Hymns on Select Passages of Holy Scripture*-1762)

Prayers, Comments & Questions

God of grace and glory, you call us with your voice of flame to be your people, faithful and courageous. As your beloved Son embraced his mission in the waters of baptism, inspire us with the fire of your Spirit to join in his transforming work. We ask this in the name of our Savior Jesus Christ, who lives and reigns for ever and ever. Amen.

January 18: Second Sunday after the Epiphany

Preparation for Sunday
Psalm 139:1-6, 13-18

Thursday
Judges 2:6-15
2 Corinthians 10:1-11

Friday
Judges 2:16-23
Acts 13:16-25

Saturday
1 Samuel 2:21-25
Matthew 25:1-13

Sunday
1 Samuel 3:1-20
Psalm 139:1-6, 13-18
1 Corinthians 6:12-20
John 1:43-51

Reflection on Sunday
Psalm 86

Monday
1 Samuel 9:27–10:8
2 Corinthians 6:14–7:1

Tuesday
1 Samuel 15:10-31
Acts 5:1-11

Wednesday
Genesis 16:1-14
Luke 18:15-17

The General Rule of Discipleship
To witness to Jesus Christ in the world and to follow his teachings
through acts of compassion, justice, worship, and devotion under the guidance of the Holy Spirit.

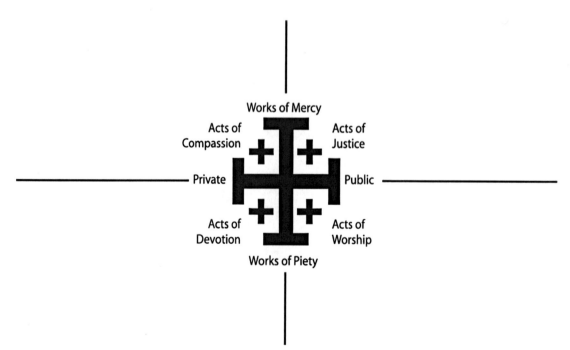

A Word from John Wesley

The very reason of the thing puts it beyond dispute, that the duty which is here enjoined is not peculiar to them, or to the Christians of the early ages. It no more regards any particular order of men, or particular time, than any particular country. No: It is of the most universal nature, respecting all times, and all persons, yea, and all things; not meats and drinks only, and things pertaining to the senses. The meaning is, "If any man," of whatever rank, station, circumstances, in any nation, in any age of the world, "will" effectually "come after me, let him deny himself" in all things; let him "take up his cross," of whatever kind; yea, and that "daily; and follow me."

A Hymn from Charles Wesley

Author of faith, eternal Word,
Whose Spirit breathes the active flame,
Faith, like its finisher and Lord,
Today as yesterday the same.

To thee our humble hearts aspire,
And ask the gift unspeakable:
Increase in us the kindled fire,
In us the work of faith fulfil.

By faith we know thee strong to save
(Save us, a present Saviour thou!)
Whate'er we hope, by faith we have,
Future and past subsisting now.

(*Collection*-1781, #92:1, 2, 3)

Prayers, Comments & Questions

Insistent God, by night and day you summon your slumbering people. So stir us with your voice and enlighten our lives with your grace that we give ourselves fully to Christ's call to mission and ministry. Amen.

January 25: Third Sunday after the Epiphany

Preparation for Sunday
Psalm 62:5-12

Thursday
Jeremiah 19:1-15
Revelation 18:11-20

Friday
Jeremiah 20:7-13
2 Peter 3:1-7

Saturday
Jeremiah 20:14-18
Luke 10:13-16

Sunday
Jonah 3:1-5, 10
Psalm 62:5-12
1 Corinthians 7:29-31
Mark 1:14-20

Reflection on Sunday
Psalm 46

Monday
Genesis 12:1-9
1 Corinthians 7:17-24

Tuesday
Genesis 45:25–46:7
Acts 5:33-42

Wednesday
Proverbs 8:1-21
Mark 3:13-19a

The General Rule of Discipleship
To witness to Jesus Christ in the world and to follow his teachings
through acts of compassion, justice, worship, and devotion under the guidance of the Holy Spirit.

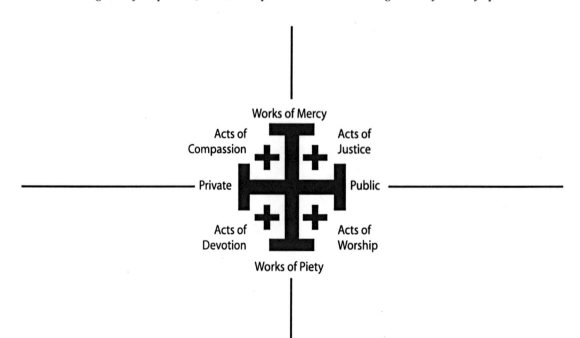

A Word from John Wesley

2. The denying ourselves, and the taking up our cross, in the full extent of the expression, is not a thing of small concern: It is not expedient only, as are some of the circumstantials of religion; but it is absolutely, indispensably necessary, either to our becoming or continuing his disciples. It is absolutely necessary, in the very nature of the thing, to our coming after Him and following Him; insomuch that, as far as we do not practise it, we are not his disciples.

A Hymn from Charles Wesley

To him that in thy name believes
Eternal life with thee is given;
Into himself he all receives—
Pardon, and holiness, and heaven.

The things unknown to feeble sense,
Unseen by reason's glimmering ray,
With strong commanding evidence
Their heavenly origin display.

Faith lends its realizing light,
The clouds disperse, the shadows fly;
Th'Invisible appears in sight,
And God is seen by mortal eye.

(*Collection*-1781, #92:4, 5, 6)

Prayers, Comments & Questions

God of the prophets, you call us from evil to serve you. Fulfill in us your commonwealth of justice and joy, that the light of your presence may be revealed to all nations, to the glory of Jesus' name. Amen.

February 1: Fourth Sunday after the Epiphany

Preparation for Sunday
Psalm 111

Thursday
Deuteronomy 3:23-29
Romans 9:6-18

Friday
Deuteronomy 12:28-32
Revelation 2:12-17

Saturday
Deuteronomy 13:1-5
Matthew 8:28–9:1

Sunday
Deuteronomy 18:15-20
Psalm 111
1 Corinthians 8:1-13
Mark 1:21-28

Reflection on Sunday
Psalm 35:1-10

Monday
Numbers 22:1-21
Acts 21:17-26

Tuesday
Numbers 22:22-28
1 Corinthians 7:32-40

Wednesday
Jeremiah 29:1-14
Mark 5:1-20

The General Rule of Discipleship
*To witness to Jesus Christ in the world and to follow his teachings
through acts of compassion, justice, worship, and devotion under the guidance of the Holy Spirit.*

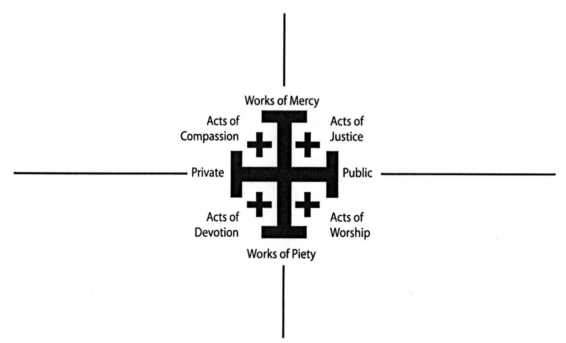

A Word from John Wesley

If we do not continually deny ourselves, we do not learn of Him, but of other masters. If we do not take up our cross daily, we do not come after Him, but after the world, or the prince of the world, or our own fleshly mind. If we are not walking in the way of the cross, we are not following Him; we are not treading in his steps; but going back from, or at least wide of, Him.

A Hymn from Charles Wesley

How can a sinner know
His sins on earth forgiven?
How can my gracious Saviour show
My name inscribed in heaven?
What we have felt and seen
With confidence we tell,
And publish to the sons of men
The signs infallible.

We who in Christ believe,
That he for us hath died,
We all his unknown peace receive,
And feel his blood applied;
Exults our rising soul,
Disburdened of her load,
And swells unutterably full
Of glory and of God.

(*Collection*-1781, #93:1 & 2)

Prayers, Comments & Questions

Holy and awesome God, your Son's authority is found in integrity and living truth, not the assertion of power over others. Open our imaginations to new dimensions of your love, and heal us of all that severs us from you and one another, that we may grow into the vision you unfold before us. Amen.

February 8: Fifth Sunday after the Epiphany

Preparation for Sunday
Psalm 147:1-11, 20c

Thursday
Proverbs 12:10-21
Galatians 5:2-15

Friday
Job 36:1-23
1 Corinthians 9:1-16

Saturday
Isaiah 46:1-13
Matthew 12:9-14

Sunday
Isaiah 40:21-31
Psalm 147:1-11, 20c
1 Corinthians 9:16-23
Mark 1:29-39

Reflection on Sunday
Psalm 102:12-28

Monday
2 Kings 4:8-17, 32-37
Acts 14:1-7

Tuesday
2 Kings 8:1-6
Acts 15:36-41

Wednesday
Job 6:1-13
Mark 3:7-12

The General Rule of Discipleship
To witness to Jesus Christ in the world and to follow his teachings
through acts of compassion, justice, worship, and devotion under the guidance of the Holy Spirit.

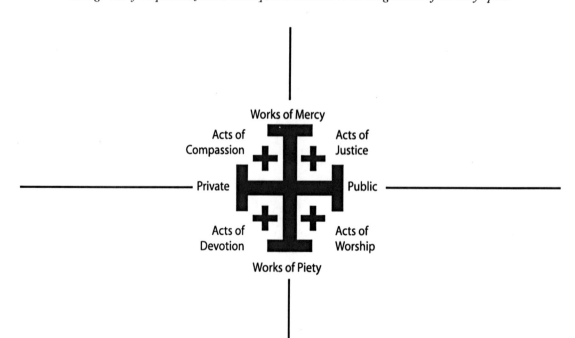

A Word from John Wesley

3. It is for this reason, that so many Ministers of Christ, in almost every age and nation, particularly since the Reformation of the Church from the innovations and corruptions gradually crept into it, have wrote and spoke so largely on this important duty, both in their public discourses and private exhortations. This induced them to disperse abroad many tracts upon the subject; and some in our own nation. They knew both from the oracles of God, and from the testimony of their own experience, how impossible it was not to deny our Master, unless we will deny ourselves; and how vainly we attempt to follow Him that was crucified, unless we take up our own cross daily.

A Hymn from Charles Wesley

His love surpassing far
The love of all beneath,
We find within our hearts, and dare
The pointless darts of death.
Stronger than death or hell
The mystic power we prove;
And conqu'rors of the world, we dwell
In heaven, who dwell in love.

We by his Spirit prove
And know the things of God;
The things which freely of his love
He hath on us bestowed:
His Spirit to us he gave,
And dwells in us, we know;
The witness in ourselves we have,
And all his fruits we show.

(*Collection*-1781, #93:3 & 4)

Prayers, Comments & Questions

Everlasting God, you give strength to the powerless and power to the faint; you raise up the sick and cast out demons. Make us agents of healing and wholeness, that your good news may be made known to the ends of your creation. Amen.

February 15: Transfiguration Sunday

Preparation for Sunday
Psalm 50:1-6

Thursday
1 Kings 11:26-40
2 Corinthians 2:12-17

Friday
1 Kings 14:1-18
1 Timothy 1:12-20

Saturday
1 Kings 16:1-7
Luke 19:41-44

Sunday
2 Kings 2:1-12
Psalm 50:1-6
2 Corinthians 4:3-6
Mark 9:2-9

Reflection on Sunday
Psalm 110:1-4

Monday
Exodus 19:7-25
Hebrews 2:1-4

Tuesday
Job 19:23-27
1 Timothy 3:14-16

Ash Wednesday
Joel 2:1-2, 12-17
Psalm 51:1-17
2 Corinthians 5:20b–6:10
Matthew 6:1-6, 16-21

The General Rule of Discipleship
*To witness to Jesus Christ in the world and to follow his teachings
through acts of compassion, justice, worship, and devotion under the guidance of the Holy Spirit.*

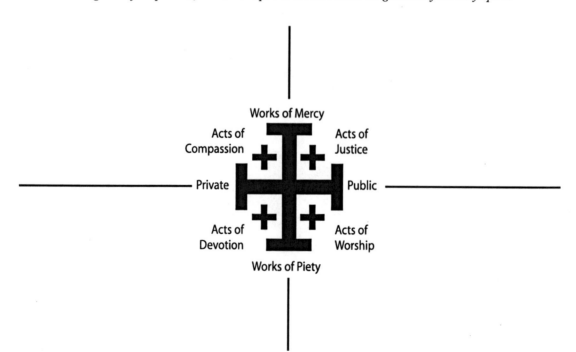

A Word from John Wesley

I. 1. I shall, First, endeavour to show, what it is for a man to "deny himself, and take up his cross daily." This is a point which is, of all others, most necessary to be considered and thoroughly understood, even on this account, that it is, of all others, most opposed by numerous and powerful enemies. All our nature must certainly rise up against this, even in its own defence; the world, consequently, the men who take nature, not grace, for their guide, abhor the very sound of it. And the great enemy of our souls, well knowing its importance, cannot but move every stone against it. But this is not all: Even those who have in some measure shaken off the yoke of the devil, who have experienced, especially of late years, a real work of grace in their hearts, yet are no friends to this grand doctrine of Christianity, though it is so peculiarly insisted on by their Master.

A Hymn from Charles Wesley

The meek and lowly heart,
That in our Saviour was,
To us his Spirit does impart,
And signs us with his cross:
Our nature's turned, our mind
Transformed in all its powers;
And both the witnesses are joined,
The Spirit of God with ours.

Whate'er our pardoning Lord
Commands, we gladly do,
And guided by his sacred Word
We all his steps pursue.
His glory our design,
We live our God to please;
And rise, with filial fear divine,
To perfect holiness.

(*Collection*-1781, #93:5 & 6)

Prayers, Comments & Questions

Holy God, mighty and immortal, you are beyond our knowing, yet we see your glory in the face of Jesus Christ, whose compassion illumines the world. Transform us into the likeness of the love of Christ, who renewed our humanity so that we may share in his divinity, the same Jesus Christ, our Lord, who lives and reigns with you and the Holy Spirit. Amen.

Lent

Preparing for Baptism and Life as a Disciple of Jesus Christ

The primary purpose of Lent from its beginnings has been to provide a period of intense formation for those preparing to take on the covenant of baptism with the baptized, with baptism celebrated at Easter. Over time, as the early church's extensive three-year system of formation (called the catechumenate) fell into disuse, Lent became in practice primarily a time for penitence and increased acts of self-discipline, as well as, in some ways, particularly among Protestants, a kind of "extended Holy Week" for contemplating the suffering of Jesus.

With the renewal of the Christian Year brought about for Roman Catholics in Vatican II and for Protestants coinciding with the development of the Revised Common Lectionary, more and more Western Christians have recovered the idea, if not entirely the practices, of Lent as a season of preparation for baptism, reconciliation for the estranged, and final preparation for confirmation or reaffirmation by those baptized who are deemed ready to take the vows of baptism for themselves for the first time or in a deeper way.

Consequently, the readings you will experience on Sundays and weekdays during Lent are much more about how Jesus teaches his disciples to follow him and not about the sufferings of Jesus or his execution per se. If your congregation is not already providing accountable small groups to read and explore the implications of these readings, Sunday and/or daily, for living as the baptized, let me encourage you to gather a few Christian friends and create your own. Consider meeting face-to-face at least once weekly.

When you gather, read one of the Gospel readings aloud three times, *lectio continua* style, paying attention the first time to what catches your attention, the second to what the thing that caught your attention is calling you to do, and the third to how you will respond in obedience to do it. Then share what you have gleaned from your reading with others in your small group, and decide how you will help one another be obedient to what you each have heard during the coming week.

Rev. Taylor Burton-Edwards

February 22: First Sunday in Lent

Preparation for Sunday
Psalm 25:1-10

Thursday
Daniel 9:1-14
1 John 1:3-10

Friday
Daniel 9:15-25a
2 Timothy 4:1-5

Saturday
Psalm 32
Matthew 9:2-13

Sunday
Genesis 9:8-17
Psalm 25:1-10
1 Peter 3:18-22
Mark 1:9-15

Reflection on Sunday
Psalm 77

Monday
Job 4:1-21
Ephesians 2:1-10

Tuesday
Job 5:8-27
1 Peter 3:8-18a

Wednesday
Proverbs 30:1-9
Matthew 4:1-11

The General Rule of Discipleship
To witness to Jesus Christ in the world and to follow his teachings
through acts of compassion, justice, worship, and devotion under the guidance of the Holy Spirit.

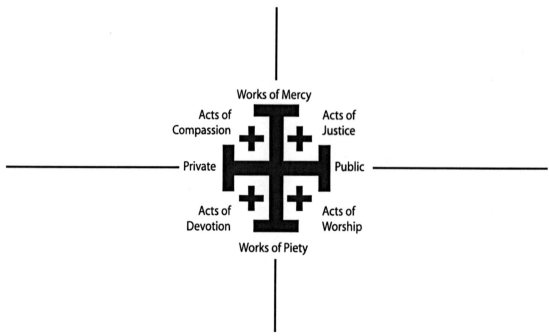

A Word from John Wesley

Some of them are as deeply and totally ignorant concerning it, as if there was not one word about it in the Bible. Others are farther off still, having unawares imbibed strong prejudices against it. These they have received partly from outside Christians, men of a fair speech and behaviour, who want nothing of godliness but the power, nothing of religion but the spirit;— and partly from those who did once, if they do not now, "taste of the powers of the world to come." But are there any of these who do not both practise self-denial themselves, and recommend it to others? You are little acquainted with mankind, if you doubt of this.

A Hymn from Charles Wesley

Fain would I know as known by thee,
And feel the indigence I see;
Fain would I all my vileness own,
And deep beneath the burden groan;
Abhor the pride that lurks within,
Detest and loathe myself and sin.

Ah, give me, Lord, myself to feel,
My total misery reveal;
Ah, give me, Lord (I still would say),
A heart to mourn, a heart to pray;
My business this, my only care,
My life, my every breath be prayer!

(*Collection*-1781, #96:4 & 5)

Prayers, Comments & Questions

God of our salvation, your bow in the clouds proclaims your covenant with every living creature. Teach us your paths and lead us in your truth, that by your Holy Spirit, we may remember our baptismal vows and be keepers of your trust with earth and its inhabitants. Amen.

March 1: Second Sunday in Lent

Preparation for Sunday
Psalm 22:23-31

Thursday
Genesis 15:1-6, 12-18
Romans 3:21-31

Friday
Genesis 16:1-6
Romans 4:1-12

Saturday
Genesis 16:7-15
Mark 8:27-30

Sunday
Genesis 17:1-7, 15-16
Psalm 22:23-31
Romans 4:13-25
Mark 8:31-38

Reflection on Sunday
Psalm 105:1-11, 37-45

Monday
Genesis 21:1-7
Hebrews 1:8-12

Tuesday
Genesis 22:1-19
Hebrews 11:1-3, 13-19

Wednesday
Jeremiah 30:12-22
John 12:36-43

The General Rule of Discipleship
*To witness to Jesus Christ in the world and to follow his teachings
through acts of compassion, justice, worship, and devotion under the guidance of the Holy Spirit.*

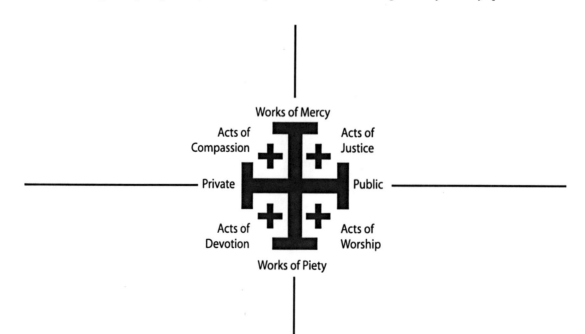

A Word from John Wesley

There are whole bodies of men who only do not declare war against it. To go no farther than London: Look upon the whole body of Predestinarians, who by the free mercy of God have lately been called out of the darkness of nature into the light of faith. Are they patterns of self-denial? How few of them even profess to practise it at all! How few of them recommend it themselves, or are pleased with them that do! Rather, do they not continually represent it in the most odious colours, as if it were seeking "salvation by works," or seeking "to establish our own righteousness?" And how readily do Antinomians of all kinds, from the smooth Moravian, to the boisterous, foul-mouthed Ranter, join the cry, with their silly, unmeaning cant of legality, and preaching the law!

A Hymn from Charles Wesley

Jesu, my heart's desire obtain!
My earnest suit present and gain,
My fullness of corruption show,
The knowledge of myself bestow;
A deeper displicence at sin,
A sharper sense of hell within,
A stronger struggling to get free,
A keener appetite for thee!

O sovereign Love, to thee I cry!
Give me thyself, or else I die!
Save me from death, from hell set free—
Death, hell, are but the want of thee.
Quickened by thy imparted flame,
Saved, when possessed of thee, I am;
My life, my only heaven thou art!
O might I feel thee in my heart!

(*Collection*-1781, #97:3 & 4)

Prayers, Comments & Questions

God of Sarah and Abraham, long ago you embraced your people in covenant and promised them your blessing. Strengthen us in faith, that, with your disciples of every age, we may proclaim your deliverance in Jesus Christ to generations yet unborn. Amen.

March 8: Third Sunday in Lent

Preparation for Sunday
Psalm 19

Thursday
Exodus 19:1-9a
1 Peter 2:4-10

Friday
Exodus 19:9b-15
Acts 7:30-40

Saturday
Exodus 19:16-25
Mark 9:2-8

Sunday
Exodus 20:1-17
Psalm 19
1 Corinthians 1:18-25
John 2:13-22

Reflection on Sunday
Psalm 84

Monday
1 Kings 6:1-4, 21-22
1 Corinthians 3:10-23

Tuesday
2 Chronicles 29:1-11, 16-19
Hebrews 9:23-28

Wednesday
Ezra 6:1-16
Mark 11:15-19

The General Rule of Discipleship
*To witness to Jesus Christ in the world and to follow his teachings
through acts of compassion, justice, worship, and devotion under the guidance of the Holy Spirit.*

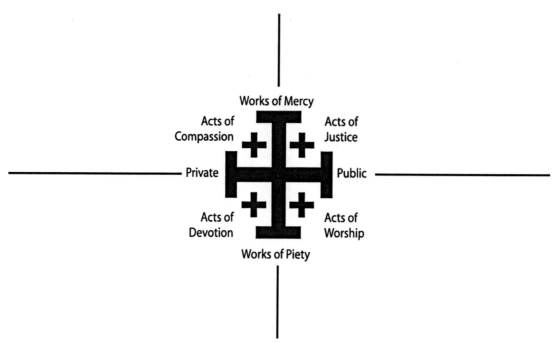

A Word from John Wesley

Therefore you are in constant danger of being wheedled, hectored, or ridiculed out of this important gospel-doctrine, either by false teachers, or false brethren, (more or less beguiled from the simplicity of the gospel,) if you are not deeply grounded therein. Let fervent prayer, then, go before, accompany, and follow what you are now about to read, that it may be written in your heart by the finger of God, so as never to be erased.

A Hymn from Charles Wesley

Saviour, Prince of Israel's race,
See me from thy lofty throne,
Give the sweet relenting grace,
Soften this obdurate stone!
Stone to flesh, O God, convert,
Cast a look and break my heart!

By thy Spirit, Lord, reprove,
All mine inmost sins reveal;
Sins against thy light and love
Let me see, and let me feel,
Sins that crucified my God,
Spilt again thy precious blood.

(*Collection*-1781, #98:1 & 2)

Prayers, Comments & Questions

Holy One, creator of the stars and seas, your steadfast love is shown to every living thing: your word calls forth countless worlds and souls; your law revives and refreshes. Forgive our misuse of your gifts, that we may be transformed by your wisdom to manifest for others the mercy of our crucified and risen Lord. Amen.

March 15: Fourth Sunday in Lent

Preparation for Sunday
Psalm 107:1-3, 17-22

Thursday
Genesis 9:8-17
Ephesians 1:3-6

Friday
Daniel 12:5-13
Ephesians 1:7-14

Saturday
Numbers 20:22-29
John 3:1-13

Sunday
Numbers 21:4-9
Psalm 107:1-3, 17-22
Ephesians 2:1-10
John 3:14-21

Reflection on Sunday
Psalm 107:1-16

Monday
Exodus 15:22-27
Hebrews 3:1-6

Tuesday
Numbers 20:1-13
1 Corinthians 10:6-13

Wednesday
Isaiah 60:15-22
John 8:12-20

The General Rule of Discipleship
To witness to Jesus Christ in the world and to follow his teachings
through acts of compassion, justice, worship, and devotion under the guidance of the Holy Spirit.

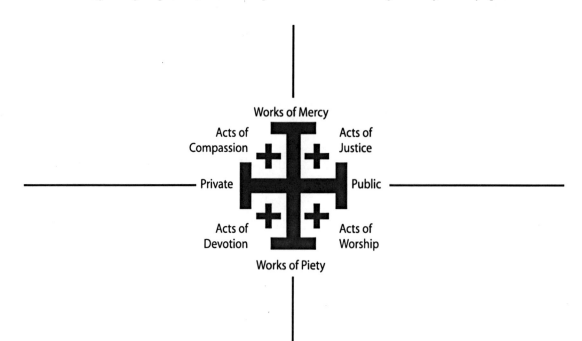

A Word from John Wesley

2. But what is self-denial? Wherein are we to deny ourselves? And whence does the necessity of this arise? I answer, The will of God is the supreme, unalterable rule for every intelligent creature; equally binding every angel in heaven, and every man upon earth. Nor can it be otherwise: This is the natural, necessary result of the relation between creatures and their Creator. But if the will of God be our one rule of action in every thing, great and small, it follows, by undeniable consequence, that we are not to do our own will in any thing.

A Hymn from Charles Wesley

O that I could repent!
With all my idols part,
And to thy gracious eye present
An humble, contrite heart!
An heart with grief oppressed
For having grieved my God;
A troubled heart, that cannot rest
Till sprinkled with thy blood!

Jesus, on me bestow
The penitent desire;
With true sincerity of woe
My aching breast inspire;
With softening pity look,
And melt my hardness down;
Strike, with thy lover's resistless stroke,
And break this heart of stone!

(*Collection*-1781, #99)

Prayers, Comments & Questions

Steadfast God, you reach out to us in mercy even when we rebel against your holy call and prefer to walk in disobedience rather than in the way of your divine truth. Soften our hearts with the warmth of your love, that we may know your Son alive within us, redeeming us and raising us up into your eternal presence. Amen.

March 22: Fifth Sunday in Lent

Preparation for Sunday
Psalm 51:1-12

Thursday
Isaiah 30:15-18
Hebrews 4:1-13

Friday
Exodus 30:1-10
Hebrews 4:14–5:4

Saturday
Habakkuk 3:2-13
John 12:1-11

Sunday
Jeremiah 31:31-34
Psalm 51:1-12
Hebrews 5:5-10
John 12:20-33

Reflection on Sunday
Psalm 119:9-16

Monday
Isaiah 43:8-13
2 Corinthians 3:4-11

Tuesday
Isaiah 44:1-8
Acts 2:14-24

Wednesday
Haggai 2:1-9, 20-23
John 12:34-50

The General Rule of Discipleship
*To witness to Jesus Christ in the world and to follow his teachings
through acts of compassion, justice, worship, and devotion under the guidance of the Holy Spirit.*

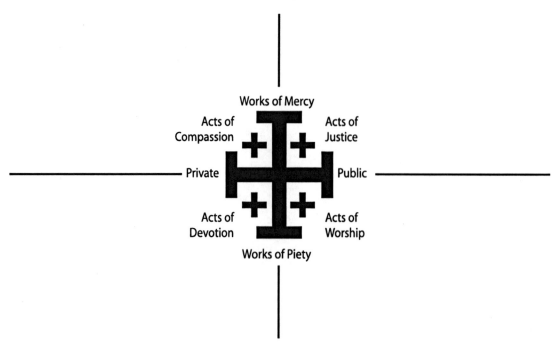

Works of Mercy

Acts of Compassion

Acts of Justice

Private

Public

Acts of Devotion

Acts of Worship

Works of Piety

A Word from John Wesley

Here, therefore, we see at once the nature, with the ground and reason, of self-denial. We see the nature of self-denial: It is the denying or refusing to follow our own will, from a conviction that the will of God is the only rule of action to us. And we see the reason thereof, because we are creatures; because "it is He that hath made us, and not we ourselves."

A Hymn from Charles Wesley

O that I could revere
My much offended God!
O that I could but stand in fear
Of thy afflicting rod!
If mercy cannot draw,
Thou, by thy threat'nings, move,
And keep an abject soul in awe
That will not yield to love.

Thou great, tremendous God,
The conscious awe impart;
The grace be now on me bestowed,
The tender, fleshly heart;
For Jesu's sake alone
The stony heart remove,
And melt at last, O melt me down
Into the mould of love.

(*Collection*-1781, #100:1 & 3)

Prayers, Comments & Questions

God of suffering and glory, in Jesus Christ you reveal the way of life through the path of obedience. Inscribe your law in our hearts, that in life we may not stray from you, but may be your people. Amen.

Holy Week

The Cost of Discipleship and Salvation

Lent proper ends and Holy Week begins with Passion/Palm Sunday. This is the time we remember the final week of Jesus in Jerusalem, his last actions with his disciples, his arrest, his trial, his torture, and his execution. The daily readings (Monday through Saturday) are the same all three years, established by long tradition. And these are readings intended to be read and reflected upon in gathered community. Many congregations will have planned gatherings for worship on Maundy Thursday and Good Friday. Fewer may be likely to gather for the solemn vigil of Holy Saturday morning or the other weekdays.

The formational power of this week is greatly enhanced if you do gather every day in some way. Perhaps you may find a time each evening to meet in homes, or a "third place," or perhaps you may decide to gather "virtually" through an online venue such as Skype, Facebook, or Twitter. While during Lent the focus of the readings was to commit to what you might do, during Holy Week the purpose is simply to let them sink in and allow the readings to work their work in your gathered community. Read the scriptures. Pray for the church and the world. And bid each other the peace of Christ. And continue to watch and pray for what the Spirit will put to death and bring to new life in each of you.

Rev. Taylor Burton-Edwards

March 29: Passion/Palm Sunday

Preparation for Sunday
Psalm 118:1-2, 19-29

Thursday
Deuteronomy 16:1-8
Philippians 2:1-11

Friday
Jeremiah 33:1-9
Philippians 2:12-18

Saturday
Jeremiah 33:10-16
Mark 10:32-34, 46-52

Sunday
Liturgy of the Palms
Psalm 118:1-2, 19-29
Mark 11:1-11

Liturgy of the Passion
Isaiah 50:4-9a
Psalm 31:9-16
Philippians 2:5-11
Mark 14:1–15:47

Monday
Isaiah 42:1-9
Psalm 36:5-11
Hebrews 9:11-15
John 12:1-11

Tuesday
Isaiah 49:1-7
Psalm 71:1-14
1 Corinthians 1:18-31
John 12:20-36

Wednesday
Isaiah 50:4-9a
Psalm 70
Hebrews 12:1-3
John 13:21-32

The General Rule of Discipleship
To witness to Jesus Christ in the world and to follow his teachings
through acts of compassion, justice, worship, and devotion under the guidance of the Holy Spirit.

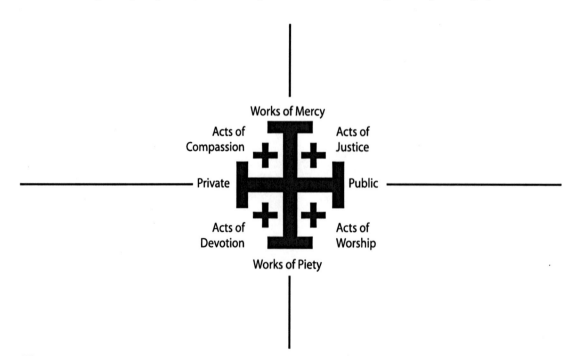

A Word from John Wesley

3. This reason for self-denial must hold, even with regard to the angels of God in heaven; and with regard to man, innocent and holy, as he came out of the hands of his Creator. But a farther reason for it arises from the condition wherein all men are since the fall. We are all now "shapen in wickedness, and in sin did our mother conceive us." Our nature is altogether corrupt, in every power and faculty. And our will, depraved equally with the rest, is wholly bent to indulge our natural corruption. On the other hand, it is the will of God that we resist and counteract that corruption, not at some times or in some things only, but at all times and in all things. Here, therefore, is a farther ground for constant and universal self-denial.

A Hymn from Charles Wesley

O Love divine! What hast thou done!
Th'immortal God hath died for me!
The Father's co-eternal Son
Bore all my sins upon the tree:
Th'immortal God for me hath died,
My Lord, my Love is crucified.

Behold him, all ye that pass by,
The bleeding Prince of life and peace!
Come see, ye worms, your Maker die,
And say, was ever grief like his?
Come, feel with me his blood applied:
My Lord, my Love is crucified.

Is crucified for me and you,
To bring us rebels back to God;
Believe, believe the record true,
Ye all are bought with Jesu's blood:
Pardon for all flows from his side:
My Lord, my Love is crucified.

Then let us sit beneath his cross,
And gladly catch the healing stream,
All things for him account but loss,
And give up all our hearts to him;
Of nothing think or speak beside,
'My Lord, my Love is crucified.'

(*Collection*-1781, #27)

Prayers, Comments & Questions

Crucified and Risen One, by your passion you sustain us when we fall knee-bent into the radical emptiness of bone-wasting sorrow and despair. Teach us to sustain the weary and awaken us to attend to those who suffer. Amen.

April 5: Resurrection of the Lord

The Three Days
Holy Thursday
Exodus 12:1-14
Psalm 116:1-2, 12-19
1 Corinthians 11:23-26
John 13:1-17, 31b-35

Good Friday
Isaiah 52:13–53:12
Psalm 22
Hebrews 10:16-25
John 18:1–19:42

Holy Saturday
Job 14:1-14
Psalm 31:1-4, 15-16
1 Peter 4:1-8
John 19:38-42

Sunday
Acts 10:34-43
Psalm 118:1-2, 14-24
1 Corinthians 15:1-11
John 20:1-18
or
Mark 16:1-8

Easter Evening
Isaiah 25:6-9
Psalm 114
1 Corinthians 5:6b-8
Luke 24:13-49

Reflection on Sunday
Psalm 118:1-2, 14-24

Monday
Genesis 1:1-19
1 Corinthians 15:35-49

Tuesday
Genesis 1:20–2:4a
1 Corinthians 15:50-58

Wednesday
Song of Solomon 3:1-11
Mark 16:1-8

The General Rule of Discipleship
To witness to Jesus Christ in the world and to follow his teachings
through acts of compassion, justice, worship, and devotion under the guidance of the Holy Spirit.

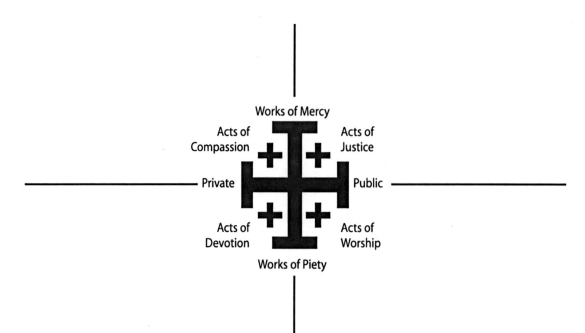

A Word from John Wesley

4. To illustrate this a little further: The will of God is a path leading straight to God. The will of man, which once ran parallel with it, is now another path, not only different from it, but, in our present state, directly contrary to it: It leads from God. If, therefore, we walk in the one, we must necessarily quit the other. We cannot walk in both. Indeed, a man of faint heart and feeble hands may go in two ways, one after the other. But he cannot walk in two ways at the same time: He cannot, at one and the same time, follow his own will, and follow the will of God: He must choose the one or the other; denying God's will, to follow his own; or denying himself, to follow the will of God.

A Hymn from Charles Wesley

Sinners, dismiss your fear,
The joyful tidings hear!
This the word that Jesus said,
O believe, and feel it true,
Christ is risen from the dead,
Lives the Lord who died for you!

Why then art thou cast down,
Thou poor afflicted one?
Full of doubts, and griefs, and fears,
Look into that open grave!
Died He not to dry thy tears?
Rose He not thy soul to save?

To purge thy guilty stain
He died, and rose again:
Wherefore does thou weep and mourn?
Sinner, lift thine heart and eye,
Turn thee, to thy Jesus turn,
See thy loving Savior nigh.

(*Hymns for Our Lord's Resurrection*-1746, #2:1, 3, & 5)

Prayers, Comments & Questions

Love divine, in raising Christ to new life you opened the path of salvation to all peoples. Send us out, with the joy of Mary Magdalene, to proclaim that we have seen the Lord, so that all the world may celebrate with you the banquet of your peace. Amen.

Easter Season

Salvation Unleashed

The first service of Easter is full of readings! This is the Great Vigil of Easter, offered after sundown on Saturday night. It is a powerful service of Fire, Word, Water, and Table. We light the new fire, signifying the light of Christ overcoming the world. We rehearse the story of God's salvation, from creation and exodus to the resurrection of Christ. We exult in Alleluias. We baptize those who have been preparing during Lent and vigiling in prayer with us during Holy Week. And we celebrate the feast of our redemption around the Lord's table. If your congregation does not yet celebrate this amazing and ancient Christian service, find one that does (most Episcopal, Roman Catholic, and many Lutheran congregations do) and take folks with you, including your pastor, so they may see, hear, smell, taste, and touch, and perhaps develop plans to bring others or create one for your congregation next year.

Easter, the Season of the Passover of our Lord, begins with a bang! And it concludes with another one, fifty days later at Pentecost, when we celebrate the coming of the Holy Spirit on the early Christians long ago, and all the ways the Spirit is moving among us here and now.

Between these days of celebration are weeks of further formation so your celebration, come Pentecost, may be full indeed. Easter Season is a time especially for helping the newly baptized with all the baptized grow in their understanding of Christian doctrine and to identify their gifts and callings for ministry in Christ's name. On Easter, both at the Great Vigil and again on Sunday morning, we exult in the resurrection of Jesus Christ from the dead. On Pentecost, we exult in what the Spirit is doing in the lives of those reborn or recommitted and bless and commission them for their ministries among us. And in the weeks between, in Sunday and in daily readings, we prepare ourselves to grow in our knowledge and love of God, and to sharpen our own passions and skills for ministry in Christ's name and the Spirit's power.

Rev. Taylor Burton-Edwards

April 12: Second Sunday of Easter

Preparation for Sunday
Psalm 133

Thursday
Daniel 1:1-21
Acts 2:42-47

Friday
Daniel 2:1-23
Acts 4:23-31

Saturday
Daniel 2:24-49
John 12:44-50

Sunday
Acts 4:32-35
Psalm 133
1 John 1:1–2:2
John 20:19-31

Reflection on Sunday
Psalm 135

Monday
Daniel 3:1-30
1 John 2:3-11

Tuesday
Daniel 6:1-28
1 John 2:12-17

Wednesday
Isaiah 26:1-15
Mark 12:18-27

The General Rule of Discipleship
To witness to Jesus Christ in the world and to follow his teachings
through acts of compassion, justice, worship, and devotion under the guidance of the Holy Spirit.

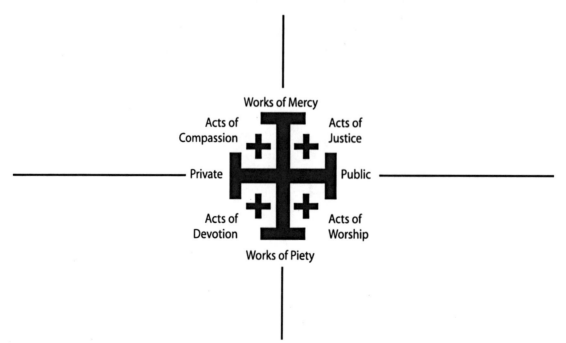

A Word from John Wesley

5. Now, it is undoubtedly pleasing, for the time, to follow our own will, by indulging, in any instance that offers, the corruption of our nature: But by following it in anything, we so far strengthen the perverseness of our will; and by indulging it, we continually increase the corruption of our nature. So, by the food which is agreeable to the palate, we often increase a bodily disease: It gratifies the taste, but it inflames the disorder; it brings pleasure, but it also brings death.

A Hymn from Charles Wesley

All ye that seek the Lord who died,
Your God for sinners crucified,
Prevent the earliest dawn, and come
To worship at his sacred tomb.

Bring the sweet spices of your sighs,
Your contrite hearts, and streaming eyes,
Your sad complaints, and humble fears;
Come, and embalm him with your tears.

While thus ye love your souls t'employ,
Your sorrow shall be turned to joy:
Now, now let all your grief be o'er
Believe, and ye shall weep no more.

Haste then, ye souls that first believe,
Who dare the Gospel-word receive,
Your faith with joyful hearts confess,
Be bold, be Jesus' witnesses.

Go tell the followers of your Lord
Their Jesus is to life restored;
He lives, that they his life may find;
He lives, to quicken all mankind.

(*Hymns for Our Lord's Resurrection*-1746, #1:1-3, 11, & 12)

Prayers, Comments & Questions

Light of the world, shine upon us and disperse the clouds of our selfishness, that we may reflect the power of the resurrection in our life together. Amen.

April 19: Third Sunday of Easter

Preparation for Sunday
Psalm 4

Thursday
Daniel 9:1-19
1 John 2:18-25

Friday
Daniel 10:2-19
1 John 2:26-28

Saturday
Acts 3:1-10
Luke 22:24-30

Sunday
Acts 3:12-19
Psalm 4
1 John 3:1-7
Luke 24:36b-48

Reflection on Sunday
Psalm 150

Monday
Jeremiah 30:1-11a
1 John 3:10-16

Tuesday
Hosea 5:15–6:6
2 John 1-6

Wednesday
Proverbs 9:1-6
Mark 16:9-18

The General Rule of Discipleship
To witness to Jesus Christ in the world and to follow his teachings
through acts of compassion, justice, worship, and devotion under the guidance of the Holy Spirit.

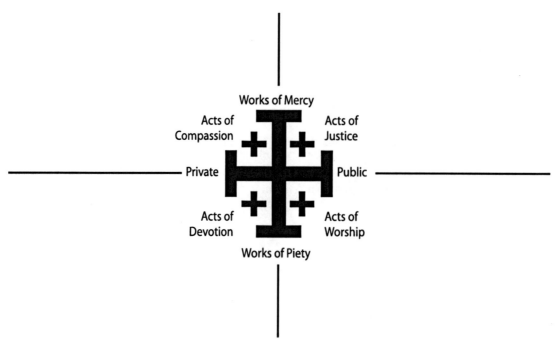

A Word from John Wesley

6. On the whole, then, to deny ourselves, is, to deny our own will, where it does not fall in with the will of God; and that however pleasing it may be. It is, to deny ourselves any pleasure which does not spring from, and lead to, God; that is, in effect, to refuse going out of our way, though into a pleasant, flowery path; to refuse what we know to be deadly poison, though agreeable to the taste.

A Hymn from Charles Wesley

Who can now presume to fear?
Who despair his Lord to see?
Show thyself alive to me?
Yes, my God, I dare not doubt,
Thou shalt all my sins remove;
Thou hast cast a legion out,
Thou wilt perfect me in Love.

Surely thou hast called me now!
Now I hear the voice divine,
At thy wounded feet I bow,
Wounded for whose sins but mine!
I have nailed him to the tree,
I have sent him to the grave:
But the Lord is risen for me,
Hold of him by faith I have.

Hear, ye brethren of the Lord,
(Such he you vouchsafes to call)
O believe the Gospel-Word,
Christ hath died, and rose for all:
Turn ye from your sins to God,
Haste to Galilee, and see
Him, who bought thee with his blood,
Him, who rose to live in thee.

(*Hymns for Our Lord's Resurrection*-1746, #3:4, 5, & 7)

Prayers, Comments & Questions

Holy and righteous God, you raised Christ from the dead and glorified him at your right hand. Let the words of scripture fulfilled in Jesus your Son, burn within our hearts and open our minds to recognize him in the breaking of bread. Amen.

April 26: Fourth Sunday of Easter

Preparation for Sunday
Psalm 23

Thursday
Genesis 30:25-43
Acts 3:17-26

Friday
Genesis 46:28–47:6
Acts 4:1-4

Saturday
Genesis 48:8-19
Mark 6:30-34

Sunday
Acts 4:5-12
Psalm 23
1 John 3:16-24
John 10:11-18

Reflection on Sunday
Psalm 95

Monday
1 Samuel 16:1-13
1 Peter 5:1-5

Tuesday
1 Chronicles 11:1-9
Revelation 7:13-17

Wednesday
Micah 7:8-20
Mark 14:26-31

The General Rule of Discipleship
To witness to Jesus Christ in the world and to follow his teachings
through acts of compassion, justice, worship, and devotion under the guidance of the Holy Spirit.

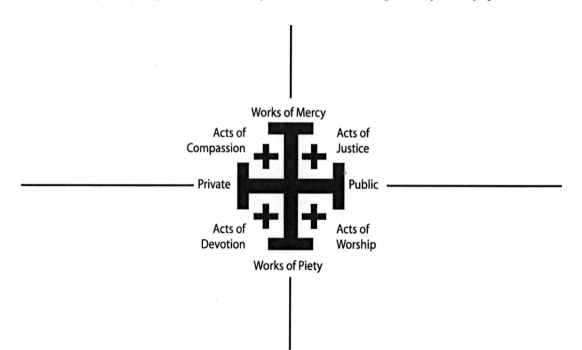

A Word from John Wesley

7. And every one that would follow Christ, that would be his real disciple, must not only deny himself, but take up his cross also. A cross is anything contrary to our will, anything displeasing to our nature. So that taking up our cross goes a little farther than denying ourselves; it rises a little higher, and is a more difficult task to flesh and blood;—it being more easy to forego pleasure, than to endure pain.

A Hymn from Charles Wesley

Jesus, the Rising Lord of all,
His Love to man commends,
Poor worms he blushes not to call
His brethren and his friends.

Who basely all forsook their Lord
In his distress, and fled,
To these he sends the joyful Word,
When risen from the dead.

Sinners, I rose again to show
Your sins are all forgiven,
And mount above the skies, that you
May follow me to Heaven.

(*Hymns for Our Lord's Resurrection*-1746, 4:1, 2, & 6)

Prayers, Comments & Questions

Shepherd of all, by laying down your life for your flock you reveal your love for all. Lead us from the place of death to the place of abundant life, that guided by your care for us, we may rightly offer our lives in love for you and our neighbors. Amen.

May 3: Fifth Sunday of Easter

Preparation for Sunday
Psalm 22:25-31

Thursday
Amos 8:1-7
Acts 8:1b-8

Friday
Amos 8:11-13
Acts 8:9-25

Saturday
Amos 9:7-15
Mark 4:30-32

Sunday
Acts 8:26-40
Psalm 22:25-31
1 John 4:7-21
John 15:1-8

Reflection on Sunday
Psalm 80

Monday
Isaiah 5:1-7
Galatians 5:16-26

Tuesday
Isaiah 32:9-20
James 3:17-18

Wednesday
Isaiah 65:17-25
John 14:18-31

The General Rule of Discipleship
To witness to Jesus Christ in the world and to follow his teachings
through acts of compassion, justice, worship, and devotion under the guidance of the Holy Spirit.

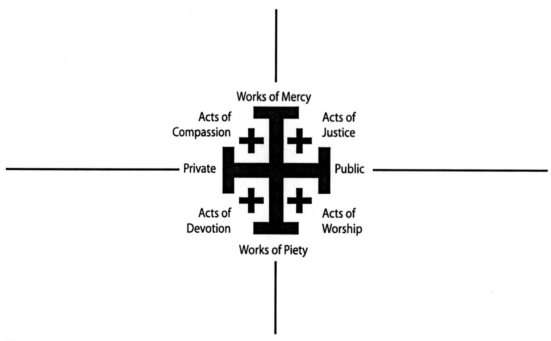

A Word from John Wesley

8. Now, in running "the race that is set before us," according to the will of God, there is often a cross lying in the way; that is, something which is not only not joyous, but grievous; something which is contrary to our will, which is displeasing to our nature. What then is to be done? The choice is plain: Either we must take up our cross, or we must turn aside from the way of God, "from the holy commandment delivered to us;" if we do not stop altogether, or turn back to everlasting perdition!

A Hymn from Charles Wesley

Object of all our knowledge here,
Our one desire, and hope below,
Jesus, the Crucified, draw near,
And with thy disciples go:
Our thoughts and words to thee are known,
We commune of thyself alone.

How can it be, our reason cries,
That God should leave his throne above?
Is it for man the Immortal dies!
For man, who tramples on his Love!
For Man, who nailed him to the tree!
O Love! O God! He dies for me!

Ah! Lord, if thou indeed art ours,
If thou for us hast burst the tomb,
Visit us with thy quickening powers,
Come to thy mournful followers come,
Thyself to thy weak members join,
And fill us with the Life Divine.

(*Hymns for Our Lord's Resurrection*-1746, #5:1, 2, & 5)

Prayers, Comments & Questions

God, you sent your Son into the world that we might live through him. May we abide in his risen life so that we may bear the fruit of love for one another and know the fullness of joy. Amen.

May 10: Sixth Sunday of Easter

Preparation for Sunday
Psalm 98

Thursday
Isaiah 49:5-6
Acts 10:1-34

Friday
Isaiah 42:5-9
Acts 10:34-43

Saturday
Deuteronomy 32:44-47
Mark 10:42-45

Sunday
Acts 10:44-48
Psalm 98
1 John 5:1-6
John 15:9-17

Reflection on Sunday
Psalm 93

Monday
Deuteronomy 7:1-11
1 Timothy 6:11-12

Tuesday
Deuteronomy 11:1-17
1 Timothy 6:13-16

Wednesday
Deuteronomy 11:18-21
Mark 16:19-20

The General Rule of Discipleship
*To witness to Jesus Christ in the world and to follow his teachings
through acts of compassion, justice, worship, and devotion under the guidance of the Holy Spirit.*

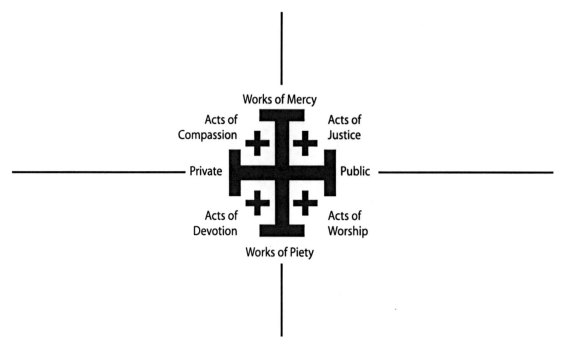

A Word from John Wesley

9. In order to the healing of that corruption, that evil disease, which every man brings with him into the world, it is often needful to pluck out, as it were, a right eye, to cut off a right hand;—so painful is either the thing itself which must be done, or the only means of doing it; the parting, suppose, with a foolish desire, with an inordinate affection; or a separation from the object of it, without which it can never be extinguished. In the former kind, the tearing away such a desire or affection, when it is deeply rooted in the soul, is often like the piercing of a sword, yea, like "the dividing asunder of the soul and spirit, the joints and marrow." The Lord then sits upon the soul as a refiner's fire, to burn up all the dross thereof. And this is a cross indeed; it is essentially painful; it must be so, in the very nature of the thing. The soul cannot be thus torn asunder, it cannot pass through the fire, without pain.

A Hymn from Charles Wesley

Come in, with thy disciples sit,
Nor suffer us to ask in vain,
Nourish us, Lord, with living meat.
Our souls with heavenly bread sustain;
Break to us now the mystic bread,
And bid us on thy body feed.

Honor the means ordained by thee,
The great unbloody sacrifice,
The deep tremendous mystery;
Thyself in our inlightened eyes
Now in the broken bread make known,
And shew us thou art all our own.

(*Hymns for Our Lord's Resurrection*-1746, #6:5 & 6)

Prayers, Comments & Questions

Faithful God, make our hearts bold with love for one another. Pour out your Spirit upon all people, that we may live your justice and sing in praise the new song of your marvelous victory. Amen.

May 17: Seventh Sunday of Easter

Preparation for Sunday
Psalm 47

Thursday,
Ascension of the Lord
Acts 1:1-11
Psalm 47
Ephesians 1:15-23
Luke 24:44-53

Friday
Exodus 24:15-18
Revelation 1:9-18

Saturday
Deuteronomy 34:1-7
John 16:4-11

Sunday
Acts 1:15-17, 21-26
Psalm 1
1 John 5:9-13
John 17:6-19

Reflection on Sunday
Psalm 115

Monday
Exodus 28:29-38
Philippians 1:3-11

Tuesday
Numbers 8:5-22
Titus 1:1-9

Wednesday
Ezra 9:5-15
John 16:16-24

The General Rule of Discipleship
To witness to Jesus Christ in the world and to follow his teachings
through acts of compassion, justice, worship, and devotion under the guidance of the Holy Spirit.

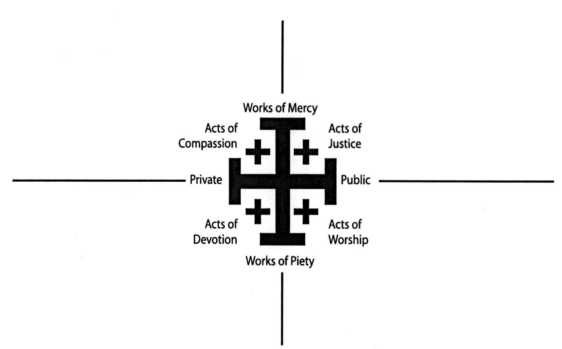

A Word from John Wesley

10. In the latter kind, the means to heal a sin-sick soul, to cure a foolish desire, an inordinate affection, are often painful, not in the nature of the thing, but from the nature of the disease. So when our Lord said to the rich young man, "Go, sell that thou hast, and give to the poor," (as well knowing, this was the only means of healing his covetousness,) the very thought of it gave him so much pain, that "he went away sorrowful;" choosing rather to part with his hope of heaven, than his possessions on earth. This was a burden he could not consent to lift, a cross he would not take up. And in the one kind or the other, every follower of Christ will surely have need to "take up his cross daily."

A Hymn from Charles Wesley

Rejoice, the Lord is King!
Your Lord and King adore,
Mortals, give thanks and sing,
And triumph evermore;
Lift up your heart, lift up your voice,
Rejoice, again, I say, Rejoice.

Jesus the Savior reigns,
The God of Truth and Love,
When he had purged our stains,
He took his seat above:
Lift up your heart, lift up your voice,
Rejoice, again, I say, rejoice.

(*Hymns for Our Lord's Resurrection*-1746, #8:1 & 2)

Prayers, Comments & Questions

Gracious God, in the resurrection of your Son Jesus Christ, you have given us eternal life and glorified your name in all the world. Refresh our souls with the living streams of your truth, that in our unity, your joy may be complete. Amen.

May 24: Day of Pentecost

Preparation for Sunday
Psalm 33:12-22

Thursday
Genesis 2:4b-7
1 Corinthians 15:42b-49

Friday
Job 37:1-13
1 Corinthians 15:50-57

Saturday
Exodus 15:6-11
John 7:37-39

Sunday
Acts 2:1-21
Psalm 104:24-34, 35b
Romans 8:22-27
John 15:26-27; 16:4b-15

Reflection on Sunday
Psalm 104:24-34, 35b

Monday
Joel 2:18-29
1 Corinthians 12:4-11

Tuesday
Genesis 11:1-9
1 Corinthians 12:12-27

Wednesday
Ezekiel 37:1-14
John 20:19-23

The General Rule of Discipleship
To witness to Jesus Christ in the world and to follow his teachings
through acts of compassion, justice, worship, and devotion under the guidance of the Holy Spirit.

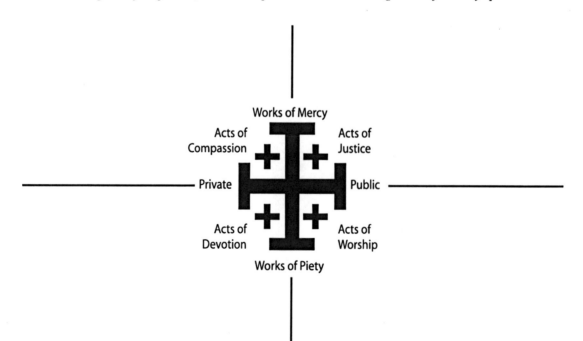

A Word from John Wesley

11. The "taking up" differs a little from "bearing his cross." We are then properly said to "bear our cross," when we endure what is laid upon us without our choice, with meekness and resignation. Whereas, we do not properly "take up our cross," but when we voluntarily suffer what it is in our power to avoid; when we willingly embrace the will of God, though contrary to our own; when we choose what is painful, because it is the will of our wise and gracious Creator.

A Hymn from Charles Wesley

Father, if justly still we claim
To us and ours the promise made,
To us be graciously the same,
And crown with living fire our head.

Our claim admit, and from above
Of holiness the spirit shower;
Of wise discernment, humble love,
And zeal, and unity, and power.

The spirit of convincing speech,
Of power demonstrative impart,
Such as may every conscience reach,
And sound the unbelieving heart.

The spirit of refining fire,
Searching the inmost of the mind,
To purge all fierce and foul desire,
And kindle life more pure and kind.

(*Collection*-1781, #444:1-4)

Prayers, Comments & Questions

Creator Spirit and Giver of life, make the dry, bleached bones of our lives live and breathe and grow again as you did of old. Pour out your Spirit upon the whole creation. Come in rushing wind and flashing fire to turn the sin and sorrow within us into faith, power, and delight. Amen.

Season after Pentecost

Living as Disciples, Embodying Salvation

This season is sometimes also referred to as "Ordinary Time," but it is intended to be far from "ordinary" in terms of its purposes in supporting and strengthening your discipleship to Jesus Christ. The word *ordinary* here actually only refers to the ordinal numbers (first, second, third, etc) used to refer to which Sunday after Pentecost a given Sunday may be through this season.

Rather than ordinary, or "ho-hum," the idea of this season is to support disciples and the whole congregation in living out the gifts and callings discerned during Easter Season and commissioned on the Day of Pentecost. In the Northern Hemisphere, this season typically corresponds with summer, when schools are out and wide varieties of vacation schedules may mean the ability to coordinate or even operate some ministries in the congregation (such as Sunday school or some choirs) may be challenged or curtailed until a re-launch in the fall. This scheduling situation makes it even more critical for congregations and individuals to make sure the profound formational and missional purposes of this season are not overlooked but intentionally planned for.

If you are using *A Disciple's Journal*, chances are you are already intent on strengthening your own discipleship. Let me encourage you to take another step. Ask your pastor to work with you to gather others who will take these months as an intentional journey of accountable discipleship and growth in ministry with you. Your congregation may not be able to provide a program for everyone that does this, but your pastor can certainly help you gather a "coalition of the willing" who will.

As you do, keep in mind that with the exceptions of Trinity Sunday and Christ the King Sunday, which begin and end this season, and All Saints, which falls during it, the three major tracks of readings (Old Testament, Epistle, and Gospel) are all semi-continuous during this season. None is intended to relate to the other, except for the "Bookend Sundays" and All Saints. The Old Testament readings are selections from the stories of the prophets, kings, and patriarchs/matriarchs (depending on the year). The Epistle readings explore the meaning and practice of the Christian life in particular early Christian communities. And the gospel readings take us on a journey through the bulk of the ministry and teaching of Jesus.

As suggested for the Season after Epiphany, you may wish to coordinate the way you and your group focus your energy and attention on the daily readings through these months with the particular stream of texts your congregation's worship leaders focus on during this time as a means to help reinforce the themes of the Sunday readings with your daily discipleship and ministry throughout these months.

Rev. Taylor Burton-Edwards

May 31: Trinity Sunday

Preparation for Sunday
Psalm 29

Thursday
Isaiah 1:1-4, 16-20
Romans 8:1-8

Friday
Isaiah 2:1-5
Romans 8:9-11

Saturday
Isaiah 5:15-24
John 15:18-20, 26-27

Sunday
Isaiah 6:1-8
Psalm 29
Romans 8:12-17
John 3:1-17

Reflection on Sunday
Psalm 20

Monday
Numbers 9:15-23
Revelation 4:1-8

Tuesday
Exodus 25:1-22
1 Corinthians 2:1-10

Wednesday
Numbers 6:22-27
Mark 4:21-25

The General Rule of Discipleship
To witness to Jesus Christ in the world and to follow his teachings
through acts of compassion, justice, worship, and devotion under the guidance of the Holy Spirit.

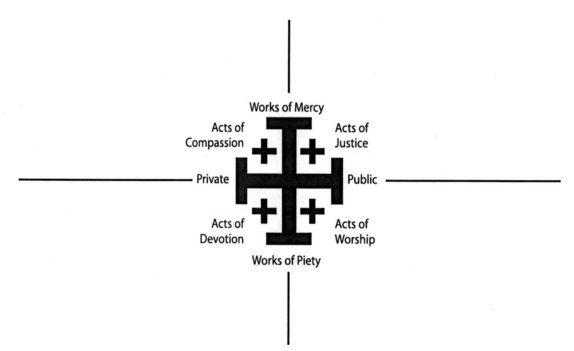

A Word from John Wesley

12. And thus it behoves every disciple of Christ to take up, as well as to bear, his cross. Indeed, in one sense, it is not his alone; it is common to him, and many others; seeing there is no temptation befalls any man, *ei me anthropinos*, "but such as is common to men;" such as is incident and adapted to their common nature and situation in the present world. But, in another sense, as it is considered with all its circumstances, it is his; peculiar to himself: It is prepared of God for him; it is given by God to him, as a token of his love. And if he receives it as such, and, after using such means to remove the pressure as Christian wisdom directs, lies as clay in the potter's hand; it is disposed and ordered by God for his good, both with regard to the quality of it, and in respect to its quantity and degree, its duration, and every other circumstance.

A Hymn from Charles Wesley

A wonderful plurality
In the true God by faith we see,
Who hear the record of the Son
"I and my Father are but One;"
In different Persons we proclaim
On God eternally the same.

Father and Son in nature join,
Each Person is alike Divine:
Alike by heaven and earth adored,
Thy Spirit makes the glorious Third:
Co-equal, co-eternal Three,
Show thyself One, great God, in me.

(*Hymns on the Trinity*-1767, #18)

Prayers, Comments & Questions

Holy God, the earth is full of the glory of your love. May we your children, born of the Spirit, so bear witness to your Son Jesus Christ, crucified and risen, that all the world may believe and have eternal life through the One who saves, Father, Son, and Holy Spirit, now and for ever. Amen.

June 7: Second Sunday after Pentecost

Preparation for Sunday
Psalm 138

Thursday
1 Samuel 4:1-22
1 Peter 4:7-19

Friday
1 Samuel 5:1-12
2 Corinthians 5:1-5

Saturday
1 Samuel 6:1-18
Luke 8:4-15

Sunday
1 Samuel 8:4-20; 11:14-15
Psalm 138
2 Corinthians 4:13–5:1
Mark 3:20-35

Reflection on Sunday
Psalm 108

Monday
1 Samuel 7:3-15
Revelation 20:1-6

Tuesday
1 Samuel 8:1-22
Revelation 20:7-15

Wednesday
1 Samuel 9:1-14
Luke 11:14-28

The General Rule of Discipleship
To witness to Jesus Christ in the world and to follow his teachings
through acts of compassion, justice, worship, and devotion under the guidance of the Holy Spirit.

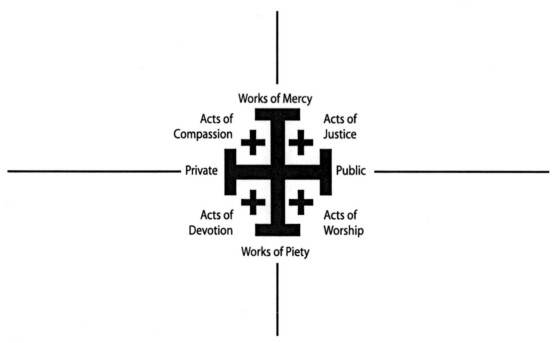

A Word from John Wesley

13. In all this, we may easily conceive our blessed Lord to act as the Physician of our souls, not merely "for his own pleasure, but for our profit, that we may be partakers of his holiness." If, in searching our wounds, he puts us to pain, it is only in order to heal them. He cuts away what is putrified or unsound, in order to preserve the sound part. And if we freely choose the loss of a limb, rather than the whole body should perish; how much more should we choose, figuratively, to cut off a right hand, rather than the whole soul should be cast into hell!

A Hymn from Charles Wesley

Now I have found the ground, wherein
Sure my soul's anchor may remain;
The wounds of Jesus, for my sin
Before the world's foundation slain:
Whose mercy shall unshaken stay
When heaven and earth are fled away.

Father, thine everlasting grace
Our scanty thought surpasses far;
Thy heart still melts with tenderness;
Thy arms of love still open are
Returning sinners to receive,
That mercy they may taste and live!

O love, thou bottomless abyss!
My sins are swallowed up in thee;
Covered is my unrighteousness,
Nor spot of guilt remains in me;
While Jesu's blood, through earth and skies,
Mercy, free, boundless mercy cries!

(*Collection*-1781, #182:1-3)

Prayers, Comments & Questions

Unlike earthly kings, you, O Lord, are ever steadfast and faithful. You sent us your Son, Jesus the Christ, to rule over us, not as a tyrant, but as a gentle shepherd. Keep us united and strong in faith, that we may always know your presence in our lives, and, when you call us home, may we enter your heavenly kingdom where you live and reign for ever and ever. Amen.

June 14: Third Sunday after Pentecost

Preparation for Sunday
Psalm 20

Thursday
1 Samuel 9:15-27
Hebrews 2:5-9

Friday
1 Samuel 10:1-8
Hebrews 11:4-7

Saturday
1 Samuel 13:1-15a
Mark 4:1-20

Sunday
1 Samuel 15:34–16:13
Psalm 20
2 Corinthians 5:6-17
Mark 4:26-34

Reflection on Sunday
Psalm 53

Monday
1 Samuel 13:23–14:23
Galatians 6:11-18

Tuesday
1 Samuel 15:10-23
Revelation 21:22–22:5

Wednesday
1 Samuel 15:24-31
Luke 6:43-45

The General Rule of Discipleship
To witness to Jesus Christ in the world and to follow his teachings
through acts of compassion, justice, worship, and devotion under the guidance of the Holy Spirit.

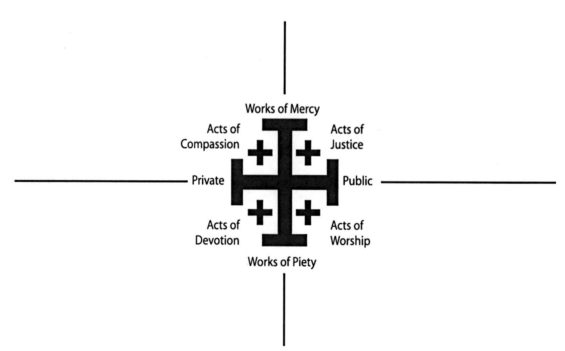

A Word from John Wesley

14. We see plainly then both the nature and ground of taking up our cross. It does not imply the disciplining ourselves, (as some speak;) the literally tearing our own flesh; the wearing hair-cloth, or iron-girdles, or anything else that would impair our bodily health; (although we know not what allowance God may make for those who act thus through involuntary ignorance;) but the embracing the will of God, though contrary to our own; the choosing wholesome, though bitter medicines; the freely accepting temporary pain, of whatever kind, and in whatever degree, when it is either essentially or accidentally necessary to eternal pleasure.

A Hymn from Charles Wesley

When darkness intercepts the skies,
And sorrow's waves around me roll,
When high the storms of passion rise,
And half o'erwhelm my sinking soul,
My soul a sudden calm shall feel,
And hear a whisper, 'Peace, be still!'

Though in affliction's furnace tried,
Unhurt on snares and deaths I'll tread;
Though sin assail, and hell thrown wide
Pour all its flames upon my head,
Like Moses' bush I'll mount the higher,
And flourish unconsumed in fire.

(*Collection*-1781, #264:6 & 7)

Prayers, Comments & Questions

Mighty God, to you belong the mysteries of the universe. You transform shepherds into kings, the smallest seeds into magnificent trees, and hardened hearts into loving ones. Bless us with your life-giving Spirit, re-create us in your image, and shape us to your purposes, through Jesus Christ. Amen.

June 21: Fourth Sunday after Pentecost

Preparation for Sunday
Psalm 9:9-20

Thursday
1 Samuel 16:14-23
Acts 20:1-16

Friday
1 Samuel 17:55–18:5
Acts 21:1-16

Saturday
1 Samuel 18:1-4
Luke 21:25-28

Sunday
1 Samuel 17:32-49
Psalm 9:9-20
2 Corinthians 6:1-13
Mark 4:35-41

Reflection on Sunday
Psalm 119:113-128

Monday
1 Samuel 18:6-30
Acts 27:13-38

Tuesday
1 Samuel 19:1-7
Acts 27:39-44

Wednesday
1 Samuel 19:8-17
Mark 6:45-52

The General Rule of Discipleship
*To witness to Jesus Christ in the world and to follow his teachings
through acts of compassion, justice, worship, and devotion under the guidance of the Holy Spirit.*

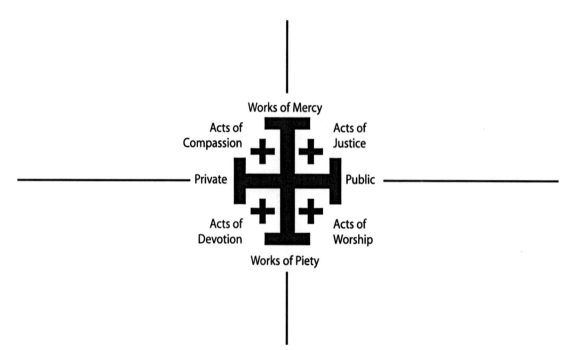

Works of Mercy

Acts of Compassion

Acts of Justice

Private

Public

Acts of Devotion

Acts of Worship

Works of Piety

A Word from John Wesley

II. 1. I am, Secondly, to show, that it is always owing to the want either of self-denial, or taking up his cross, that any man does not thoroughly follow Him, is not fully a disciple of Christ.

It is true, this may be partly owing, in some cases, to the want of the means of grace; of hearing the true word of God spoken with power; of the sacraments, or of Christian fellowship. But where none of these is wanting, the great hinderance of our receiving or growing in the grace of God is always the want of denying ourselves, or taking up our cross.

A Hymn from Charles Wesley

Come, O my guilty brethren, come,
Groaning beneath your load of sin;
His bleeding heart shall make you room,
His open side shall take you in.
He calls you now, invites you home—
Come, O my guilty brethren, come.

For you the purple current flowed
In pardons from his wounded side;
Languished for you th'eternal God,
For you the Prince of glory died.
Believe, and all your sin's forgiven,
Only believe—and yours is heaven!

(*Collection*-1781, #29:6 & 7)

Prayers, Comments & Questions

God our protector, you stood by David in the time of trial. Stand with us through all life's storms, giving us courage to risk danger to protect those who are oppressed and poor, that they may know you as their stronghold and hope. Amen.

June 28: Fifth Sunday after Pentecost

Preparation for Sunday
Psalm 130

Thursday
1 Samuel 19:18-24
2 Corinthians 7:2-16

Friday
1 Samuel 20:1-25
2 Corinthians 8:1-7

Saturday
1 Samuel 20:27-42
Luke 4:31-37

Sunday
2 Samuel 1:1, 17-27
Psalm 130
2 Corinthians 8:7-15
Mark 5:21-43

Reflection on Sunday
Psalm 18:1-6, 43-50

Monday
1 Samuel 23:14-18
2 Corinthians 8:16-24

Tuesday
1 Samuel 31:1-13
2 Corinthians 9:1-5

Wednesday
1 Chronicles 10:1-14
Mark 9:14-29

The General Rule of Discipleship
To witness to Jesus Christ in the world and to follow his teachings
through acts of compassion, justice, worship, and devotion under the guidance of the Holy Spirit.

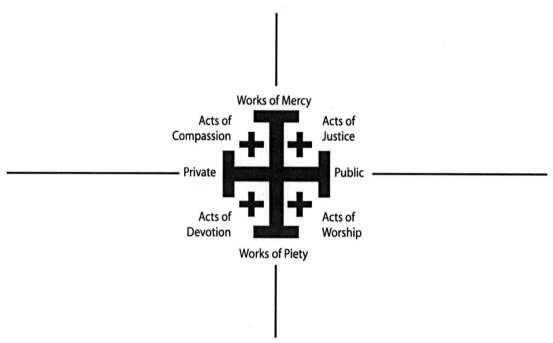

A Word from John Wesley

2. A few instances will make this plain. A man hears the word which is able to save his soul: He is well pleased with what he hears, acknowledges the truth, and is a little affected by it; yet he remains "dead in trespasses and sins," senseless and unawakened. Why is this? Because he will not part with his bosom-sin, though he now knows it is an abomination to the Lord. He came to hear, full of lust and unholy desire; and he will not part with them. Therefore no deep impression is made upon him, but his foolish heart is still hardened: That is, he is still senseless and unawakened, because he will not deny himself.

A Hymn from Charles Wesley

What though my shrinking flesh complain
And murmur to contend so long?
I rise superior to my pain:
When I am weak, then I am strong;
And when my all of strength shall fail
I shall with the God-man prevail.

Yield to me now—for I am weak,
But confident in self-despair!
Speak to my heart, in blessings speak,
Be conquered by my instant prayer:
Speak, or thou never hence shalt move,
And tell me if thy name is LOVE.

(*Collection*-1781, #136:5 & 6)

Prayers, Comments & Questions

God of hope, you are ruler of night as well as day, guardian of those who wander in the shadows. Be new light and life for those who live in the darkness of despair, for prisoners of guilt and grief, for victims of fantasy and depression, that even where death's cold grip tightens, we may know the power of the one who conquered fear and death. Amen.

July 5: Sixth Sunday after Pentecost

Preparation for Sunday
Psalm 48

Thursday
2 Samuel 2:1-11
1 Corinthians 4:8-13

Friday
2 Samuel 3:1-12
2 Corinthians 10:7-11

Saturday
2 Samuel 3:31-38
Matthew 8:18-22

Sunday
2 Samuel 5:1-5, 9-10
Psalm 48
2 Corinthians 12:2-10
Mark 6:1-13

Reflection on Sunday
Psalm 21

Monday
2 Samuel 5:1-10
2 Corinthians 11:16-33

Tuesday
2 Samuel 5:11-16
James 5:7-12

Wednesday
2 Samuel 5:17-25
John 7:1-9

The General Rule of Discipleship
To witness to Jesus Christ in the world and to follow his teachings
through acts of compassion, justice, worship, and devotion under the guidance of the Holy Spirit.

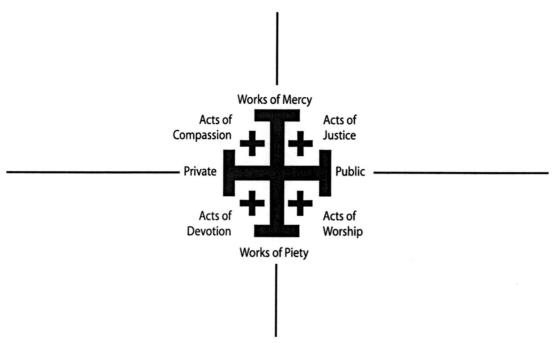

Works of Mercy

Acts of Compassion   Acts of Justice

Private   Public

Acts of Devotion   Acts of Worship

Works of Piety

A Word from John Wesley

3. Suppose he begins to awake out of sleep, and his eyes are a little opened, why are they so quickly closed again? Why does he again sink into the sleep of death? Because he again yields to his bosom-sin; he drinks again of the pleasing poison. Therefore it is impossible that any lasting impression should be made upon his heart: That is, he relapses into his fatal insensibility, because he will not deny himself.

A Hymn from Charles Wesley

Prophet, to me reveal
Thy Father's perfect will:
Never mortal spake like thee,
Human prophet like divine;
Loud and strong their voices be,
Small, and still, and inward thine!

On thee my Priest I call,
Thy blood atoned for all:
Still the Lamb as slain appears,
Still thou stand'st before the throne,
Ever off'ring up my prayers,
These presenting with thy own.

Jesu, thou art my King,
From thee my strength I bring:
Shadowed by thy mighty hand,
Saviour, who shall pluck me thence?
Faith supports, by faith I stand,
Strong as thy omnipotence.

(*Collection*-1781, #186:6-8)

Prayers, Comments & Questions

Guardian of the weak, through the teachings of your prophets you have claimed our cities, towns, and homes as temples of your presence and citadels of your justice. Turn the places we live into strongholds of your grace, that the most vulnerable as well as the most powerful among us may find peace in the security that comes in the strong name of Jesus Christ. Amen.

July 12: Seventh Sunday after Pentecost

Preparation for Sunday
Psalm 24

Thursday
Exodus 25:10-22
Colossians 2:1-5

Friday
Exodus 37:1-16
Colossians 4:2-18

Saturday
Numbers 10:11-36
Luke 1:57-80

Sunday
2 Samuel 6:1-5, 12b-19
Psalm 24
Ephesians 1:3-14
Mark 6:14-29

Reflection on Sunday
Psalm 68:24-35

Monday
2 Samuel 6:6-12a
Acts 21:27-39

Tuesday
2 Samuel 3:12-16
Acts 23:12-35

Wednesday
2 Samuel 6:16-23
Luke 7:31-35

The General Rule of Discipleship
*To witness to Jesus Christ in the world and to follow his teachings
through acts of compassion, justice, worship, and devotion under the guidance of the Holy Spirit.*

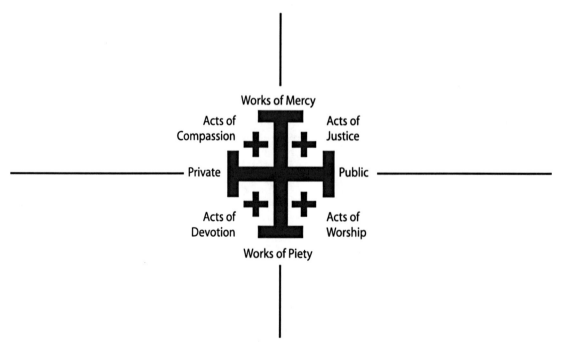

A Word from John Wesley

4. But this is not the case with all. We have many instances of those who when once awakened sleep no more. The impressions once received do not wear away: They are not only deep, but lasting. And yet, many of these have not found what they seek: They mourn, and yet are not comforted. Now, why is this? It is because they do not "bring forth fruits meet for repentance;" because they do not, according to the grace they have received, "cease from evil, and do good." They do not cease from the easily besetting sin, the sin of their constitution, of their education, or of their profession; or they omit doing the good they may, and know they ought to do, because of some disagreeable circumstances attending it: That is, they do not attain faith, because they will not "deny themselves," or "take up their cross."

A Hymn from Charles Wesley

Regard me with a gracious eye,
The long-sought blessing give,
And bid me, at the point to die,
Behold thy face and live.

A darker soul did never yet
Thy promised help implore;
O, that I now my Lord might meet,
And never lose him more!

Now, Jesus, now the Father's love
Shed in my heart abroad,
The middle wall of sin remove,
And let me into God!

(*Collection*-1781, #113:4-6)

Prayers, Comments & Questions

God of hosts, before whom David danced and sang, Mother of mercy and Father of our Lord Jesus Christ, in whom all things cohere: whenever we are confronted by lust, hate, or fear, give us the faith of John the baptizer, that we may trust in the redemption of your Messiah. Amen.

July 19: Eighth Sunday after Pentecost

Preparation for Sunday
Psalm 89:20-37

Thursday
1 Chronicles 11:15-19
Colossians 1:15-23

Friday
1 Chronicles 14:1-2
Acts 17:16-31

Saturday
1 Chronicles 15:1-2,
16:4-13
Luke 18:35-43

Sunday
2 Samuel 7:1-14a
Psalm 89:20-37
Ephesians 2:11-22
Mark 6:30-34, 53-56

Reflection on Sunday
Psalm 61

Monday
2 Samuel 7:18-29
Hebrews 13:17-25

Tuesday
2 Samuel 8:1-18
Acts 20:17-38

Wednesday
2 Samuel 9:1-13
Luke 15:1-7

The General Rule of Discipleship
To witness to Jesus Christ in the world and to follow his teachings
through acts of compassion, justice, worship, and devotion under the guidance of the Holy Spirit.

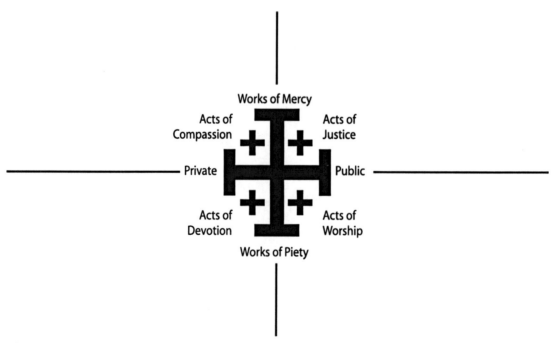

A Word from John Wesley

5. But this man did receive "the heavenly gift;" he did "taste of the powers of the world to come;" he saw "the light of the glory of God in the face of Jesus Christ;" the "peace which passeth all understanding" did rule his heart and mind; and "the love of God was shed abroad" therein, "by the Holy Ghost which was given unto him;"—yet he is now weak as another man; he again relishes the things of earth, and has more taste for the things which are seen than for those which are not seen; the eye of his understanding is closed again, so that he cannot "see Him that is invisible;" his love is waxed cold, and the peace of God no longer rules in his heart. . . .

A Hymn from Charles Wesley

Holy Lamb, who thee confess,
Followers of thy holiness,
Thee they ever keep in view,
Ever ask, 'What shall we do?'

Governed by thy only will,
All thy words we would fulfil,
Would in all thy footsteps go,
Walk as Jesus walked below.

While thou didst on earth appear,
Servant to thy servants here,
Mindful of thy place above,
All thy life was prayer and love.

(*Collection*-1781, #515:1-3)

Prayers, Comments & Questions

Holy God of Israel, ever present and moving among your people, draw us near to you, that in place of hostility there may be peace; in place of loneliness, compassion; in place of aimlessness, direction; and in place of sickness, healing; through Christ Jesus, in whom you draw near to us. Amen.

July 26: Ninth Sunday after Pentecost

Preparation for Sunday
Psalm 14

Thursday
2 Samuel 10:1-5
Colossians 1:9-14

Friday
2 Samuel 10:6-12
Colossians 3:12-17

Saturday
2 Samuel 10:13-19
John 4:31-38

Sunday
2 Samuel 11:1-15
Psalm 14
Ephesians 3:14-21
John 6:1-21

Reflection on Sunday
Psalm 37:12-22

Monday
2 Samuel 11:14-21
Philippians 4:10-20

Tuesday
2 Samuel 11:22-27
Romans 15:22-33

Wednesday
2 Chronicles 9:29-31
Mark 6:35-44

The General Rule of Discipleship
To witness to Jesus Christ in the world and to follow his teachings
through acts of compassion, justice, worship, and devotion under the guidance of the Holy Spirit.

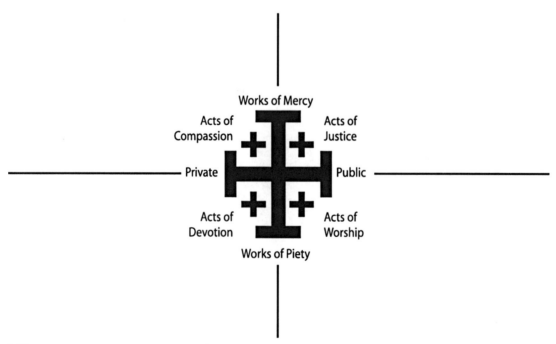

Works of Mercy

Acts of Compassion   Acts of Justice

Private   Public

Acts of Devotion   Acts of Worship

Works of Piety

A Word from John Wesley

. . . And no marvel; for he has again given place to the devil, and grieved the Holy Spirit of God. He has turned again unto folly, to some pleasing sin, if not in outward act, yet in heart. He has given place to pride, or anger, or desire, to self-will, or stubbornness. Or he did not stir up the gift of God which was in him; he gave way to spiritual sloth, and would not be at the pains of "praying always, and watching thereunto with all perseverance:" That is, he made shipwreck of the faith, for want of self-denial, and taking up his cross daily.

A Hymn from Charles Wesley

Christ, my Master and my Lord,
Let me thy forerunner be;
O be mindful of thy word,
Visit them, and visit me!
To this house, and all herein,
Now let thy salvation come!
Save our souls from inbred sin,
Make us thy eternal home!

Let us never, never rest
Till the promise is fulfilled;
Till we are of thee possessed,
Pardoned, sanctified, and sealed;
Till we all, in love renewed,
Find the pearl that Adam lost,
Temples of the living God,
Father, Son, and Holy Ghost.

(*Collection*-1781, #467:2 & 3)

Prayers, Comments & Questions

In your compassionate love, O God, you nourish us with the words of life and bread of blessing. Grant that Jesus may calm our fears and move our hearts to praise your goodness by sharing our bread with others. Amen.

August 2: Tenth Sunday after Pentecost

Preparation for Sunday
Psalm 51:1-12

Thursday
Exodus 32:19-26a
1 Corinthians 11:17-22

Friday
Joshua 23:1-16
1 Corinthians 11:27-34

Saturday
Judges 6:1-10
Matthew 16:5-12

Sunday
2 Samuel 11:26–12:13a
Psalm 51:1-12
Ephesians 4:1-16
John 6:24-35

Reflection on Sunday
Psalm 50:16-23

Monday
2 Samuel 12:15-25
Ephesians 4:17-24

Tuesday
2 Samuel 13:1-19
1 Corinthians 12:27-31

Wednesday
2 Samuel 13:20-36
Mark 8:1-10

The General Rule of Discipleship
To witness to Jesus Christ in the world and to follow his teachings
through acts of compassion, justice, worship, and devotion under the guidance of the Holy Spirit.

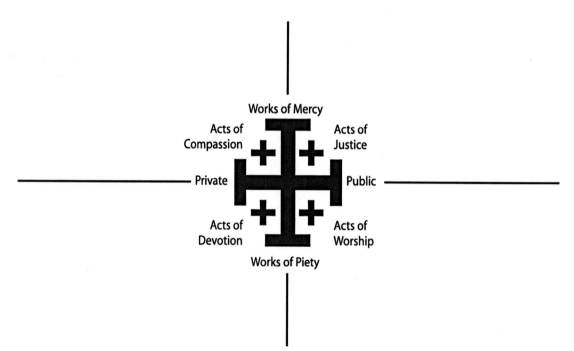

A Word from John Wesley

6. But perhaps he has not made shipwreck of the faith: He has still a measure of the Spirit of adoption, which continues to witness with his spirit that he is a child of God. However, he is not "going on to perfection;" he is not, as once, hungering and thirsting after righteousness, panting after the whole image and full enjoyment of God, as the hart after the water-brook. Rather he is weary and faint in his mind, and, as it were, hovering between life and death. And why is he thus, but because he hath forgotten the word of God, "By works is faith made perfect?"

A Hymn from Charles Wesley

Give me, Lord, the victory,
My heart's desire fulfil;
Let it now be done to me
According to thy will!
Give me living bread to eat,
And say, in answer to my call,
Canaanite, thy faith is great!
My grace is free for all.

If thy grace for all is free,
Thy call now let me hear;
Show this token upon me,
And bring salvation near.
Now the gracious word repeat,
The word of healing to my soul:
Canaanite, thy faith is great!
Thy faith hath made thee whole.

(*Collection*-1781, #158:5 & 6)

Prayers, Comments & Questions

God of the lowly and the mighty, you know the ugliness of your people when we harm and destroy one another, yet you offer us forgiveness of our sins if we but turn to you. Expand our hearts to receive the mercy you give us, that, in turn, we may share your grace and mercy with others each moment of our lives. Amen.

August 9: Eleventh Sunday after Pentecost

Preparation for Sunday
Psalm 130

Thursday
2 Samuel 13:37–14:24
Romans 15:1-6

Friday
2 Samuel 14:25-33
Galatians 6:1-10

Saturday
2 Samuel 15:1-13
Matthew 7:7-11

Sunday
2 Samuel 18:5-9, 15, 31-33
Psalm 130
Ephesians 4:25–5:2
John 6:35, 41-51

Reflection on Sunday
Psalm 57

Monday
2 Samuel 15:13-31
Ephesians 5:1-14

Tuesday
2 Samuel 18:19-33
2 Peter 3:14-18

Wednesday
2 Samuel 19:1-18
John 6:35-40

The General Rule of Discipleship
To witness to Jesus Christ in the world and to follow his teachings
through acts of compassion, justice, worship, and devotion under the guidance of the Holy Spirit.

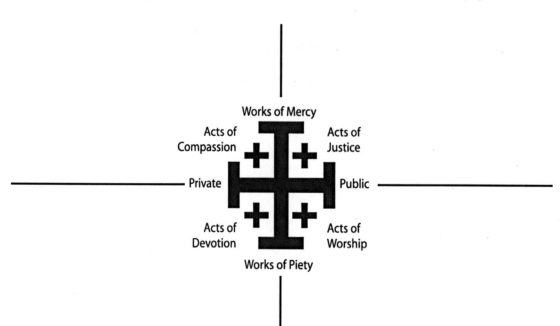

A Word from John Wesley

He does not use all diligence in working the works of God. He does not "continue instant in prayer," private as well as public; in communicating, hearing, meditation, fasting, and religious conference. If he does not wholly neglect some of these means, at least he does not use them all with his might. Or he is not zealous of works of charity, as well as works of piety. He is not merciful after his power, with the full ability which God giveth. He does not fervently serve the Lord by doing good to men, in every kind and in every degree he can, to their souls as well as their bodies. And why does he not continue in prayer?

A Hymn from Charles Wesley

Lay thy weighty cross on me,
All my unbelief control;
Till the rebel cease to be,
Keep him down within my soul;
That he never more may move,
Root and ground me fast in love.

Give me faith to hold me up,
Walking over life's rough sea;
Holy, purifying hope
Still my soul's sure anchor be;
That I may be always thine,
Perfect me in love divine.

(*Collection*-1781, #176:3 & 4)

Prayers, Comments & Questions

Bread of heaven, you feed us in the depths of grief, sin, and hostility. Nourish us with your word through the long hours of tears, and in the dawning awareness of our need for forgiveness, so that we may be redeemed by your steadfast love. Amen.

August 16: Twelfth Sunday after Pentecost

Preparation for Sunday
Psalm 111

Thursday
1 Kings 1:1-30
Acts 6:8-15

Friday
1 Kings 1:28-48
Romans 16:17-20

Saturday
1 Kings 2:1-11
John 4:7-26

Sunday
1 Kings 2:10-12; 3:3-14
Psalm 111
Ephesians 5:15-20
John 6:51-58

Reflection on Sunday
Psalm 101

Monday
1 Kings 3:16-28
Acts 6:1-7

Tuesday
1 Kings 7:1-12
Acts 7:9-16

Wednesday
1 Kings 8:1-21
Mark 8:14-21

The General Rule of Discipleship

*To witness to Jesus Christ in the world and to follow his teachings
through acts of compassion, justice, worship, and devotion under the guidance of the Holy Spirit.*

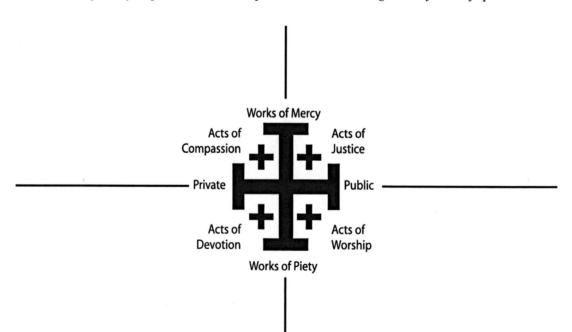

A Word from John Wesley

Because in times of dryness it is pain and grief unto him. He does not continue in hearing at all opportunities, because sleep is sweet; or it is cold, or dark, or rainy. But why does he not continue in works of mercy? Because he cannot feed the hungry, or clothe the naked, unless he retrench the expense of his own apparel, or use cheaper and less pleasing food. Beside which, the visiting the sick, or those that are in prison, is attended with many disagreeable circumstances. And so are most works of spiritual mercy; reproof, in particular.

A Hymn from Charles Wesley

Lord, regard my earnest cry,
A potsherd of the earth,
A poor, guilty worm am I,
A Canaanite by birth.
Save me from this tyranny,
From all the power of Satan save;
Mercy, mercy upon me,
Thou Son of David, have!

To the sheep of Israel's fold
Thou in thy flesh wast sent;
Yet the Gentiles now behold
In thee their covenant.
See me then, with pity see,
A sinner whom thou cam'st to save!
Mercy, mercy, upon me,
Thou Son of David, have!

(*Collection*-1781, #158:1 & 2)

Prayers, Comments & Questions

Living God, you are the giver of wisdom and true discernment, guiding those who seek your ways to choose the good. Mercifully grant that your people, feasting on the true bread of heaven, may have eternal life in Jesus Christ our Lord. Amen.

August 23: Thirteenth Sunday after Pentecost

Preparation for Sunday
Psalm 84

Thursday
1 Kings 4:20-28
1 Thessalonians 5:1-11

Friday
1 Kings 4:29-34
Romans 13:11-14

Saturday
1 Kings 5:1-12
Luke 11:5-13

Sunday
1 Kings 8:22-30, 41-43
Psalm 84
Ephesians 6:10-20
John 6:56-69

Reflection on Sunday
Psalm 11

Monday
1 Kings 5:13-18
Ephesians 5:21–6:9

Tuesday
1 Kings 6:1-14
Ephesians 6:21-24

Wednesday
1 Kings 6:15-38
John 15:16-25

The General Rule of Discipleship
*To witness to Jesus Christ in the world and to follow his teachings
through acts of compassion, justice, worship, and devotion under the guidance of the Holy Spirit.*

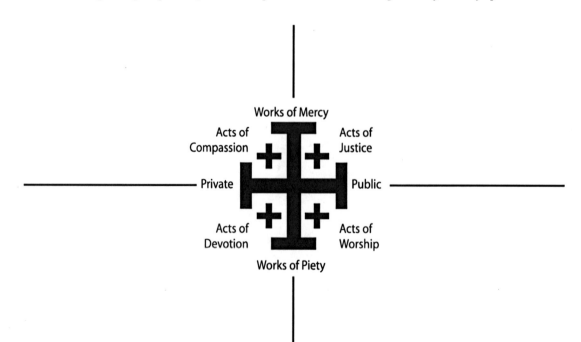

A Word from John Wesley

He would reprove his neighbour; but sometimes shame, sometimes fear, comes between: For he may expose himself, not only to ridicule, but to heavier inconveniences too. Upon these and the like considerations, he omits one or more, if not all, works of mercy and piety. Therefore, his faith is not made perfect, neither can he grow in grace; namely, because he will not deny himself, and take up his daily cross.

A Hymn from Charles Wesley

How happy then are we,
Who build, O Lord, on thee!
What can our foundation shock?
Though the shattered earth remove,
Stands our city on a rock,
On the rock of heavenly love.

A house we call our own,
Which cannot be o'erthrown:
In the general ruin sure,
Storms and earthquakes it defies,
Built immovably secure,
Built eternal in the skies.

(*Collection*-1781, #65:2 & 3)

Prayers, Comments & Questions

Gracious God, although we once were strangers, you receive us as friends and draw us home to you. Set your living bread before us that, feasting around your table, we may be strengthened to continue the work to which your Son commissioned us. Amen.

August 30: Fourteenth Sunday after Pentecost

Preparation for Sunday
Psalm 45:1-2, 6-9

Thursday
Song of Solomon 1:1-17
James 1:1-8

Friday
Song of Solomon 2:1-7
James 1:9-16

Saturday
Hosea 3:1-5
John 18:28-32

Sunday
Song of Solomon 2:8-13
Psalm 45:1-2, 6-9
James 1:17-27
Mark 7:1-8, 14-15, 21-23

Reflection on Sunday
Psalm 144:9-15

Monday
Song of Solomon 3:6-11
1 Timothy 4:6-16

Tuesday
Song of Solomon 5:2–6:3
1 Peter 2:19-25

Wednesday
Song of Solomon 8:5-7
Mark 7:9-23

The General Rule of Discipleship
To witness to Jesus Christ in the world and to follow his teachings
through acts of compassion, justice, worship, and devotion under the guidance of the Holy Spirit.

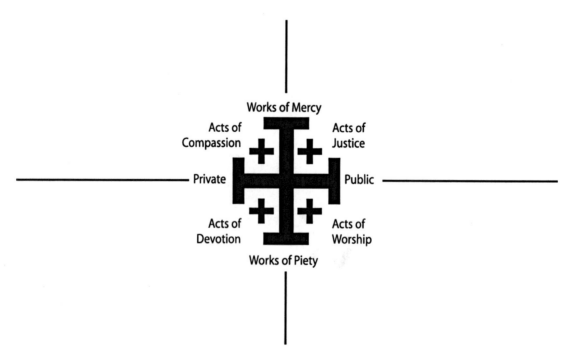

A Word from John Wesley

7. It manifestly follows, that it is always owing to the want either of self-denial, or taking up his cross, that a man does not thoroughly follow his Lord, that he is not fully a disciple of Christ. It is owing to this, that he who is dead in sin does not awake, though the trumpet be blown; that he who begins to awake out of sleep, yet has no deep or lasting conviction; that he who is deeply and lastingly convinced of sin does not attain remission of sins; that some who have received this heavenly gift retain it not, but make shipwreck of the faith; and that others, if they do not draw back to perdition, yet are weary and faint in their mind, and do not reach the mark of the prize of the high calling of God in Christ Jesus.

A Hymn from Charles Wesley

Pain and sickness, at thy word,
And sin and sorrow flies;
Speak to me, Almighty Lord,
And bid my spirit rise!
Bid me take my burden up,
The bed on which thyself didst lie,
When on Calvary's steep top
My Jesus deigned to die.

Bid me bear the hallowed cross
Which thou hast borne before,
Walk in all thy righteous laws,
And go, and sin no more.
Jesus, I on thee alone
For persevering grace depend!
Love me freely, love thine own,
And love me to the end!

(*Collection*-1781, #160:6 & 7)

Prayers, Comments & Questions

Blessed are you, O Lord and Lover, source of beauty and depth of passion. Strengthen and inspire us to do the word we hear and live the faith we confess. Amen.

September 6: Fifteenth Sunday after Pentecost

Preparation for Sunday
Psalm 125

Thursday
Proverbs 1:1-9
Romans 2:1-11

Friday
Proverbs 4:10-27
Romans 2:12-16

Saturday
Proverbs 8:1-31
Matthew 15:21-31

Sunday
Proverbs 22:1-2, 8-9, 22-23
Psalm 125
James 2:1-17
Mark 7:24-37

Reflection on Sunday
Psalm 73:1-20

Monday
Proverbs 8:32–9:6
Hebrews 11:29–12:2

Tuesday
Proverbs 11:1-31
Hebrews 12:3-13

Wednesday
Proverbs 14:1-9
Matthew 17:14-21

The General Rule of Discipleship
*To witness to Jesus Christ in the world and to follow his teachings
through acts of compassion, justice, worship, and devotion under the guidance of the Holy Spirit.*

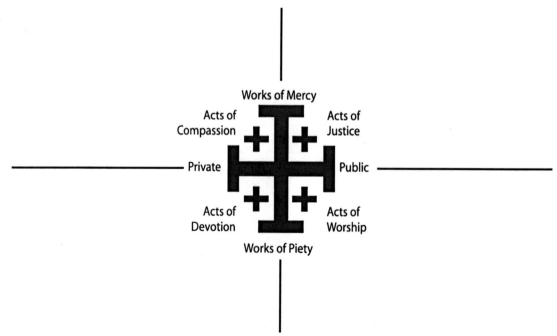

A Word from John Wesley

III. 1. How easily may we learn hence, that they know neither the Scripture nor the power of God, who directly or indirectly, in public or in private, oppose the doctrine of self denial and the daily cross! How totally ignorant are these men of an hundred particular texts, as well as of the general tenor of the whole oracles of God! And how entirely unacquainted must they be with true, genuine, Christian experience;—of the manner wherein the Holy Spirit ever did, and does at this day, work in the souls of men! They may talk, indeed, very loudly and confidently, (a natural fruit of ignorance,) as though they were the only men who understood either the word of God, or the experience of his children; but their words are, in every sense, vain words; they are weighed in the balance, and found wanting.

A Hymn from Charles Wesley

Eternal Wisdom, thee we praise,
Thee the creation sings;
With thy loud name, rocks, hills, and seas,
And heaven's high palace rings.

Thy hand, how wide it spreads the sky!
How glorious to behold!
Tinged with a blue of heavenly dye,
And starred with sparkling gold.

There thou hast bid the globes of light
Their endless circles run;
There the pale planet rules the night,
The day obeys the sun.

If down I turn my wond'ring eyes
On clouds and storms below,
Those under-regions of the skies
Thy num'rous glories show.

(*Collection*-1781, #217:1-4)

Prayers, Comments & Questions

Holy Lord, maker of us all, you call us to love our neighbors as ourselves and teach us that faith without works is dead. Open us to the opportunities for ministry that lie before us, where faith and works and the need of our neighbor come together in the name of Jesus Christ, our Savior. Amen.

September 13: Sixteenth Sunday after Pentecost

Preparation for Sunday
Psalm 19

Thursday
Proverbs 15:1-17
Hebrews 11:17-22

Friday
Proverbs 19:24-29
James 2:17-26

Saturday
Proverbs 21:1-17
Matthew 21:23-32

Sunday
Proverbs 1:20-33
Psalm 19
James 3:1-12
Mark 8:27-38

Reflection on Sunday
Psalm 73:21-28

Monday
Proverbs 22:1-21
Romans 3:9-20

Tuesday
Proverbs 25:1-28
Colossians 3:1-11

Wednesday
Proverbs 29:1-27
John 7:25-36

The General Rule of Discipleship
To witness to Jesus Christ in the world and to follow his teachings
through acts of compassion, justice, worship, and devotion under the guidance of the Holy Spirit.

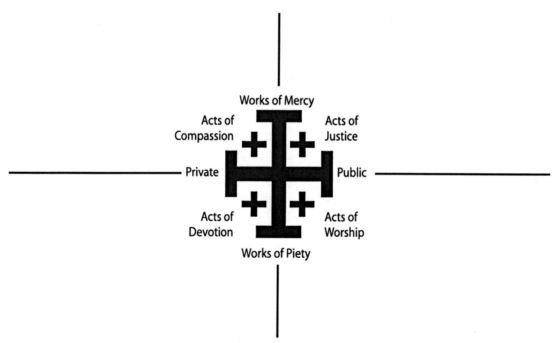

A Word from John Wesley

2. We may learn from hence, Secondly, the real cause why not only many particular persons, but even bodies of men, who were once burning and shining lights, have now lost both their light and heat. If they did not hate and oppose, they at least lightly esteemed, this precious gospel doctrine. If they did not boldly say, "We trample all self-denial under foot, we devote it to destruction;" yet they neither valued it according to its high importance, nor took any pains in practising it. *Hanc mystici docent*, said that great, bad man: "The mystic writers teach self-denial."—No; the inspired writers! And God teaches it to every soul who is willing to hear his voice!

A Hymn from Charles Wesley

The noisy winds stand ready there
Thy orders to obey;
With sounding wings they sweep the air
To make thy chariot way.

There like a trumpet, loud and strong,
Thy thunder shakes our coast;
While the red lightnings wave along
The banners of thy host.

On the thin air, without a prop,
Hang fruitful showers around;
At thy command they sink, and drop
Their fatness on the ground.

Lo! here thy wondrous skill arrays
The earth in cheerful green;
A thousand herbs thy art displays,
A thousand flowers between.

(*Collection*-1781, #217:5-8)

Prayers, Comments & Questions

Wisdom of God, from the street corners and at the entrances to the city you proclaim the way of life and of death. Grant us the wisdom to recognize your Messiah, that following in the way of the cross, we may know the way of life and glory. Amen.

September 20: Seventeenth Sunday after Pentecost

Preparation for Sunday
Psalm 1

Thursday
Proverbs 30:1-10
1 Corinthians 2:1-5

Friday
Proverbs 30:18-33
Romans 11:25-32

Saturday
Ecclesiastes 1:1-18
Matthew 23:29-39

Sunday
Proverbs 31:10-31
Psalm 1
James 3:13–4:3, 7-8a
Mark 9:30-37

Reflection on Sunday
Psalm 128

Monday
Proverbs 27:1-27
James 4:8-17

Tuesday
Ecclesiastes 4:9-16
James 5:1-6

Wednesday
Ecclesiastes 5:1-20
John 8:21-38

The General Rule of Discipleship
To witness to Jesus Christ in the world and to follow his teachings
through acts of compassion, justice, worship, and devotion under the guidance of the Holy Spirit.

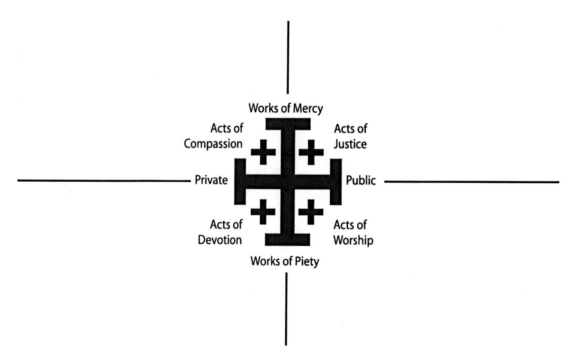

A Word from John Wesley

3. We may learn from hence, Thirdly, that it is not enough for a Minister of the gospel not to oppose the doctrine of self-denial, to say nothing concerning it. Nay, he cannot satisfy his duty by saying a little in favour of it. If he would, indeed, be pure from the blood of all men, he must speak of it frequently and largely; he must inculcate the necessity of it in the clearest and strongest manner; he must press it with his might, on all persons, at all times, and in all places; laying "line upon line, line upon line, precept upon precept, precept upon precept:" So shall he have a conscience void of offence; so shall he save his own soul and those that hear him.

A Hymn from Charles Wesley

There the rough mountains of the deep
Obey thy strong command;
Thy breath can raise the billows steep,
Or sink them to the sand.

Thy glories blaze all nature round,
And strike the wond'ring sight,
Through skies, and seas, and solid ground,
With terror and delight.

Infinite strength and equal skill
Shine through thy works abroad;
Our souls with vast amazement fill,
And speak the builder God!

But the mild glories of thy grace
Our softer passions move;
Pity divine in Jesu's face
We see, adore, and love!

(*Collection*-1781, #217:9-12)

Prayers, Comments & Questions

God of unsearchable mystery and light, your weakness is greater than our strength, your foolishness brings all our cleverness to naught, your gentleness confounds the power we would claim. You call first to be last and last to be first, servant to be leader and ruler to be underling of all. Pour into our hearts the wisdom of your Word and Spirit, that we may know your purpose and live to your glory. Amen.

September 27: Eighteenth Sunday after Pentecost

Preparation for Sunday
Psalm 124

Thursday
Esther 1:1-21
Acts 4:13-31

Friday
Esther 2:1-23
Acts 12:20-25

Saturday
Esther 3:1-15
Matthew 5:13-20

Sunday
Esther 7:1-6, 9-10; 9:20-23
Psalm 124
James 5:13-20
Mark 9:38-50

Reflection on Sunday
Psalm 140

Monday
Esther 4:1-17
1 Peter 1:3-9

Tuesday
Esther 5:1-14
1 John 2:18-25

Wednesday
Esther 8:1-17
Matthew 18:6-9

The General Rule of Discipleship
To witness to Jesus Christ in the world and to follow his teachings
through acts of compassion, justice, worship, and devotion under the guidance of the Holy Spirit.

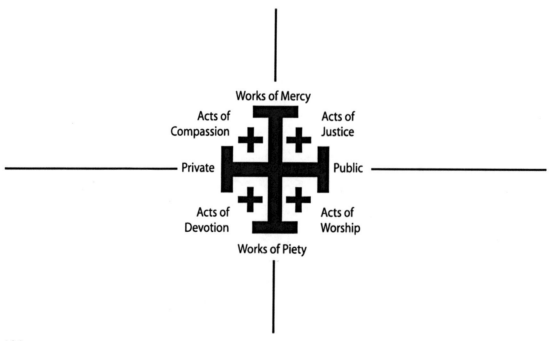

A Word from John Wesley

4. Lastly: See that you apply this, every one of you, to your own soul. Meditate upon it when you are in secret: Ponder it in your heart! Take care not only to understand it thoroughly, but to remember it to your lives' end! Cry unto the Strong for strength, that you may no sooner understand, than enter upon the practice of it! Delay not the time, but practise it immediately, from this very hour! Practise it universally, on every one of the thousand occasions which occur in all circumstances of life! Practise it daily, without intermission, from the hour you first set your hand to the plough, and enduring therein to the end, till your spirit returns to God!

A Hymn from Charles Wesley

Summoned my labour to renew,
And glad to act my part,
Lord, in thy name my work I do,
And with a single heart.

End of my every action thou,
In all things thee I see;
Accept my hallowed labour now;
I do it unto thee.

Whate'er the Father views as thine
He views with gracious eyes;
Jesu, this mean oblation join
To thy great sacrifice.

(*Collection*-1781, #312:1-3)

Prayers, Comments & Questions

O God, our guide and help in alien and contentious places: as Esther prayed faithfully and worked courageously for the deliverance of your people, strengthen us to confront the oppressor and free the oppressed, so that all people may know the justice and unity of your realm. Amen.

October 4: Nineteenth Sunday after Pentecost

Preparation for Sunday
Psalm 26

Thursday
Job 2:11–3:26
Galatians 3:23-29

Friday
Job 4:1-21
Romans 8:1-11

Saturday
Job 7:1-21
Luke 16:14-18

Sunday
Job 1:1; 2:1-10
Psalm 26
Hebrews 1:1-4; 2:5-12
Mark 10:2-16

Reflection on Sunday
Psalm 55:1-15

Monday
Job 8:1-22
1 Corinthians 7:1-9

Tuesday
Job 11:1-20
1 Corinthians 7:10-16

Wednesday
Job 15:1-35
Matthew 5:27-36

The General Rule of Discipleship
*To witness to Jesus Christ in the world and to follow his teachings
through acts of compassion, justice, worship, and devotion under the guidance of the Holy Spirit.*

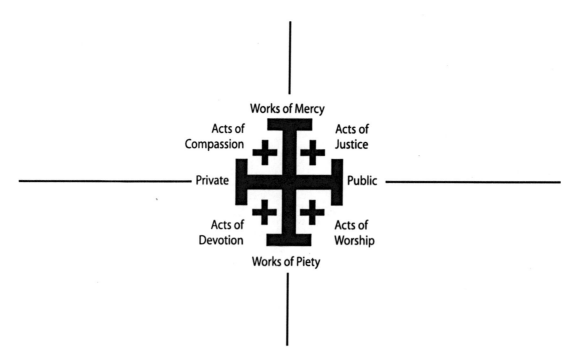

A Word from John Wesley

It may be needful to specify whom I mean by this ambiguous term; since it would be lost labour to speak to Methodists, so called, without first describing those to whom I speak. By Methodists I mean, a people who profess to pursue (in whatsoever measure they have attained) holiness of heart and life, inward and outward conformity in all things to the revealed will of God; who place religion in an uniform resemblance of the great object of it; in a steady imitation of Him they worship, in all his imitable perfections; more particularly, in justice, mercy, and truth, or universal love filling the heart, and governing the life.

"Advice to the People Called Methodists"

A Hymn from Charles Wesley

God of almighty love,
By whose sufficient grace
I lift my heart to things above,
And humbly seek thy face;
Through Jesus Christ the just
My faint desires receive,
And let me in thy goodness trust,
And to thy glory live.

Spirit of faith, inspire
My consecrated heart;
Fill me with pure, celestial fire,
With all thou hast and art;
My feeble mind transform,
And, perfectly renewed,
Into a saint exalt a worm—
A worm exalt to God!

(*Collection*-1781, #314:1& 3)

Prayers, Comments & Questions

Mighty and powerful God, through Jesus Christ our Savior you come to save people in all times and places, offering them new life in your presence. Give us open hearts to receive your Chosen One, that through him we may dwell with you as faithful and committed disciples. Amen.

October 11: Twentieth Sunday after Pentecost

Preparation for Sunday
Psalm 22:1-15

Thursday
Job 17:1-16
Hebrews 3:7-19

Friday
Job 18:1-21
Hebrews 4:1-11

Saturday
Job 20:1-29
Matthew 15:1-9

Sunday
Job 23:1-9, 16-17
Psalm 22:1-15
Hebrews 4:12-16
Mark 10:17-31

Reflection on Sunday
Psalm 39

Monday
Job 26:1-14
Revelation 7:9-17

Tuesday
Job 28:12–29:10
Revelation 8:1-5

Wednesday
Job 32:1-22
Luke 16:19-31

The General Rule of Discipleship
To witness to Jesus Christ in the world and to follow his teachings
through acts of compassion, justice, worship, and devotion under the guidance of the Holy Spirit.

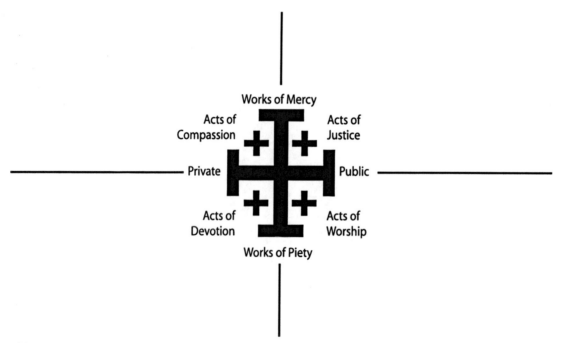

Works of Mercy

Acts of Compassion — Acts of Justice

Private — Public

Acts of Devotion — Acts of Worship

Works of Piety

A Word from John Wesley

You, to whom I now speak, believe this love of human kind cannot spring but from the love of God. You think there can be no instance of one whose tender affection embraces every child of man, (though not endeared to him either by ties of blood, or by any natural or civil relation,) unless that affection flow from a grateful, filial love to the common Father of all; to God, considered not only as his Father, but as "the Father of the spirits of all flesh;" yea, as the general Parent and Friend of all the families both of heaven and earth.

"Advice to the People Called Methodists"

A Hymn from Charles Wesley

O thou who camest from above
The pure celestial fire t'impart,
Kindle a flame of sacred love
On the mean altar of my heart!

There let it for thy glory burn
With inextinguishable blaze,
And trembling to its source return
In humble love, and fervent praise.

Jesu, confirm my heart's desire
To work, and speak, and think for thee;
Still let me guard the holy fire,
And still stir up thy gift in me;

Ready for all thy perfect will,
My acts of faith and love repeat,
Till death thy endless mercies seal,
And make the sacrifice complete.

(*Collection*-1781, #318)

Prayers, Comments & Questions

God, you promise never to forsake us, but to bring us to life, nurture us with your presence, and sustain us even in the hour of our death. Meet us in our deepest doubts when we feel abandoned, drowning in our fear of your absence. Visit us in the tension between our yearning and our anger, that we may know your mercy and grace in our time of need. Amen.

October 18: Twenty-First Sunday after Pentecost

Preparation for Sunday
Psalm 104:1-9, 24, 35c

Thursday
Job 36:1-16
Romans 15:7-13

Friday
Job 37:1-24
Revelation 17:1-18

Saturday
Job 39:1-30
Luke 22:24-30

Sunday
Job 38:1-7, 34-41
Psalm 104:1-9, 24, 35c
Hebrews 5:1-10
Mark 10:35-45

Reflection on Sunday
Psalm 75

Monday
Job 40:1-24
Hebrews 6:1-12

Tuesday
Job 41:1-11
Hebrews 6:13-20

Wednesday
Job 41:12-34
John 13:1-17

The General Rule of Discipleship
To witness to Jesus Christ in the world and to follow his teachings
through acts of compassion, justice, worship, and devotion under the guidance of the Holy Spirit.

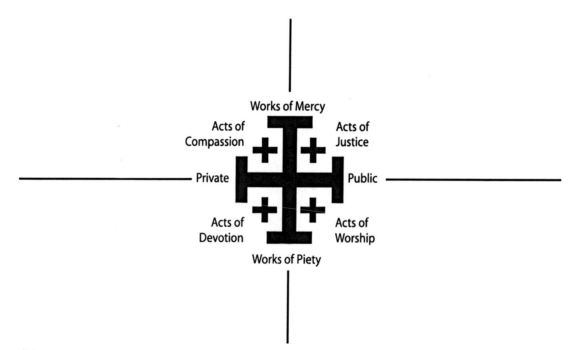

A Word from John Wesley

You suppose this faith to imply an evidence that God is merciful to me a sinner; that he is reconciled to me by the death of his Son, and now accepts me for his sake. You accordingly describe the faith of a real Christian as "a sure trust and confidence" (over and above his assent to the sacred writings) "which he hath in God, that his sins are forgiven; and that he is, through the merits of Christ, reconciled to the favour of God."

"Advice to the People Called Methodists"

A Hymn from Charles Wesley

Forth in thy name, O Lord, I go,
My daily labour to pursue,
Thee, only thee, resolved to know
In all I think, or speak, or do.

The task thy wisdom has assigned
O let me cheerfully fulfill,
In all my works thy presence find,
And prove thy acceptable will.

Thee may I set at my right hand
Whose eyes my inmost substance see,
And labour on at thy command,
And offer all my works to thee.

Give me to bear thy easy yoke,
And every moment watch and pray,
And still to things eternal look,
And hasten to thy glorious day.

For thee delightfully employ
Whate'er thy bounteous grace hath given,
And run my course with even joy,
And closely walk with thee to heaven.

(*Collection*-1781, #315:1-5)

Prayers, Comments & Questions

Creator God, you are wrapped in light as a garment, clothed with honor and majesty. Enlighten us with true faith and humble obedience that seeks to serve others in your name. Amen.

October 25: Twenty-Second Sunday after Pentecost

Preparation for Sunday
Psalm 34:1-8, 19-22

Thursday
2 Kings 20:12-19
Hebrews 7:1-10

Friday
Nehemiah 1:1-11
Hebrews 7:11-22

Saturday
Job 42:7-9
Mark 8:22-26

Sunday
Job 42:1-6, 10-17
Psalm 34:1-8, 19-22
Hebrews 7:23-28
Mark 10:46-52

Reflection on Sunday
Psalm 28

Monday
Isaiah 59:9-19
1 Peter 2:1-10

Tuesday
Ezekiel 18:1-32
Acts 9:32-35

Wednesday
Ezekiel 14:12-23
Matthew 20:29-34

The General Rule of Discipleship
To witness to Jesus Christ in the world and to follow his teachings
through acts of compassion, justice, worship, and devotion under the guidance of the Holy Spirit.

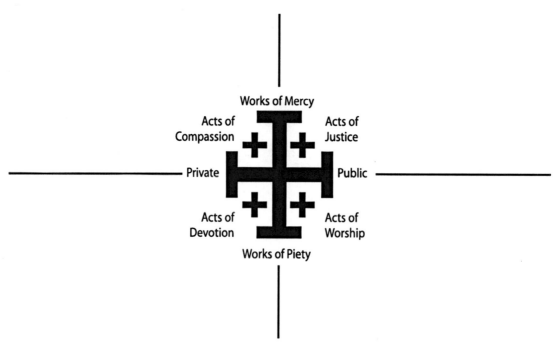

A Word from John Wesley

You believe, farther, that both this faith and love are wrought in us by the Spirit of God; nay, that there cannot be in any man one good temper or desire, or so much as one good thought, unless it be produced by the almighty power of God, by the inspiration or influence of the Holy Ghost. If you walk by this rule, continually endeavouring to know and love and resemble and obey the great God and Father of our Lord Jesus Christ, as the God of love, of pardoning mercy; if from this principle of loving, obedient faith, you carefully abstain from all evil, and labour, as you have opportunity, to do good to all men, friends or enemies; if, lastly, you unite together, to encourage and help each other in thus working out your salvation, and for that end watch over one another in love, you are they whom I mean by Methodists.

"Advice to the People Called Methodists"

A Hymn from Charles Wesley

Try us, O God, and search the ground
Of every sinful heart!
Whate'er of sin in us is found,
O bid it all depart!

When to the right or left we stray,
Leave us not comfortless,
But guide our feet into the way
Of everlasting peace.

Help us to help each other, Lord,
Each other's cross to bear;
Let each his friendly aid afford,
And feel his brother's care.

Help us to build each other up,
Our little stock improve;
Increase our faith, confirm our hope,
And perfect us in love.

(*Collection*-1781, #489:1-4)

Prayers, Comments & Questions

Almighty God, creator of heaven and earth in whom all things are possible, have mercy on us and heal us, that sustained by the power of your word and by the constant intercession of our Lord and Savior, we may draw near to you and follow in your way as faithful disciples. Amen.

November 1: Twenty-Third Sunday after Pentecost

Preparation for Sunday
Psalm 146

Thursday
Ruth 1:18-22
Hebrews 9:1-12

Friday
Ruth 2:1-9
Romans 3:21-31

Saturday
Ruth 2:10-14
Luke 10:25-37

Sunday
Ruth 1:1-18
Psalm 146
Hebrews 9:11-14
Mark 12:28-34

Reflection on Sunday
Psalm 18:20-30

Monday
Ruth 2:15-23
Romans 12:17-21; 13:8-10

Tuesday
Ruth 3:1-7
Acts 7:17-29

Wednesday
Ruth 3:8-18
John 13:31-35

The General Rule of Discipleship
To witness to Jesus Christ in the world and to follow his teachings
through acts of compassion, justice, worship, and devotion under the guidance of the Holy Spirit.

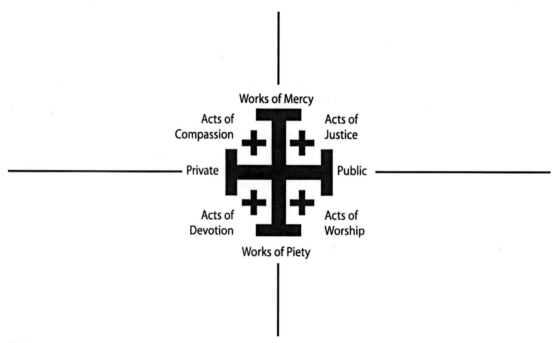

A Word from John Wesley

So much stress you lay even on right opinions, as to profess, that you earnestly desire to have a right judgment in all things, and are glad to use every means which you know or believe may be conducive thereto; and yet not so much as to condemn any man upon earth, merely for thinking otherwise than you do; much less, to imagine that God condemns him for this, if he be upright and sincere of heart.

"Advice to the People Called Methodists"

A Hymn from Charles Wesley

Jesu, united by thy grace,
And each to each endeared,
With confidence we seek thy face,
And know our prayer is heard.

Still let us own our common Lord,
And bear thine easy yoke,
A band of love, a threefold cord
Which never can be broke.

Make us into one Spirit drink,
Baptize into thy name,
And let us always kindly think,
And sweetly speak the same.

Touched by the loadstone of thy love,
Let all our hearts agree,
And ever towards each other move,
And ever move towards thee.

(*Collection*-1781, #490:1-4)

Prayers, Comments & Questions

Beloved Companion, you deal with us kindly in steadfast love, lifting up those bent low with care and sustaining the weak and oppressed. Release us from our anxious fears, that we, holding fast to your commandments, may honor you with all that we are and all that we have. Amen.

November 8: Twenty-Fourth Sunday after Pentecost

Preparation for Sunday
Psalm 127

Thursday
Ruth 4:1-10
Romans 5:6-11

Friday
Ruth 4:11-17
Hebrews 9:15-24

Saturday
Ruth 4:18-22
Mark 11:12-14, 20-24

Sunday
Ruth 3:1-5; 4:13-17
Psalm 127
Hebrews 9:24-28
Mark 12:38-44

Reflection on Sunday
Psalm 113

Monday
Genesis 24:1-10
1 Timothy 5:1-8

Tuesday
Genesis 24:11-27
1 Timothy 5:9-16

Wednesday
Genesis 24:28-42
Luke 4:16-30

The General Rule of Discipleship
To witness to Jesus Christ in the world and to follow his teachings
through acts of compassion, justice, worship, and devotion under the guidance of the Holy Spirit.

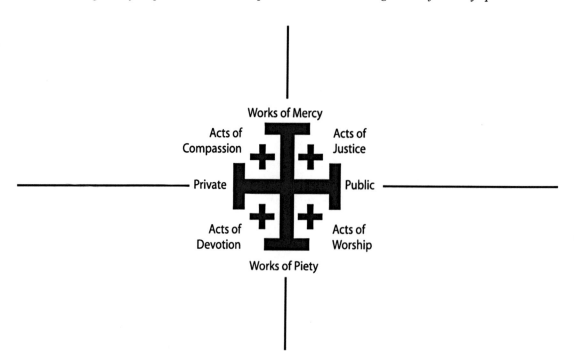

A Word from John Wesley

"Consider deeply with yourself, Is the God whom I serve able to deliver me? I am not able to deliver myself out of these difficulties; much less am I able to bear them. I know not how to give up my reputation, my friends, my substance, my liberty, my life. Can God give me to rejoice in doing this; and may I depend upon him that he will? Are the hairs of my head all numbered; and does He never fail them that trust in him?" Weigh this thoroughly; and if you can trust God with your all, then go on in the power of his might.

"Advice to the People Called Methodists"

A Hymn from Charles Wesley

To thee inseparably joined,
Let all our spirits cleave;
O may we all the loving mind
That was in thee receive!

This is the bond of perfectness,
Thy spotless charity;
O let us (still we pray) possess
The mind that was in thee!

Grant this, and then from all below
Insensibly remove;
Our souls their change shall scarcely know,
Made perfect first in love!

With ease our souls through death shall glide
Into their paradise,
And thence on wings of angels ride
Triumphant through the skies.

Yet when the fullest joy is given,
The same delight we prove,
In earth, in paradise, in heaven
Our all in all is love.

(*Collection*-1781, #490:5-9)

Prayers, Comments & Questions

God our redeemer, in sustaining the lives of Naomi and Ruth, you gave new life to your people. We ask that from age to age, new generations may be born to restore life and nourish the weak, by returning to you those things we once thought ours. Amen.

November 15: Twenty-Fifth Sunday after Pentecost

Preparation for Sunday
1 Samuel 2:1-10

Thursday
1 Samuel 1:21-28
1 Timothy 6:11-21

Friday
1 Samuel 2:18-21
Colossians 2:6-15

Saturday
1 Samuel 3:1-18
Mark 12:1-12

Sunday
1 Samuel 1:4-20
1 Samuel 2:1-10
Hebrews 10:11-25
Mark 13:1-8

Reflection on Sunday
Psalm 3

Monday
1 Samuel 3:19–4:2
Hebrews 10:26-31

Tuesday
Deuteronomy 26:5-10
Hebrews 10:32-39

Wednesday
1 Kings 8:22-30
Mark 13:9-23

The General Rule of Discipleship

To witness to Jesus Christ in the world and to follow his teachings
through acts of compassion, justice, worship, and devotion under the guidance of the Holy Spirit.

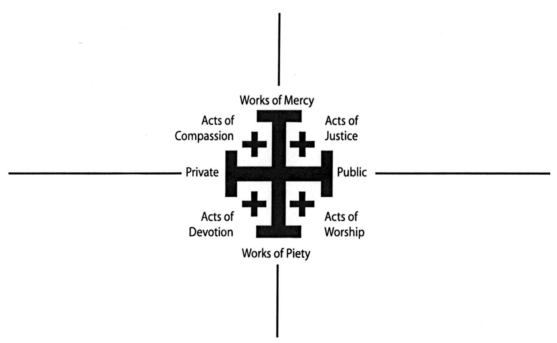

A Word from John Wesley

"Keep in the very path wherein you now tread. Be true to your principles." Never rest again in the dead formality of religion. Pursue with your might inward and outward holiness; a steady imitation of Him you worship; a still increasing resemblance of his imitable perfections, his justice, mercy, and truth.

"Advice to the People Called Methodists"

A Hymn from Charles Wesley

Jesu, thou art our King,
To me thy succour bring.
Christ, the mighty one art thou,
Help for all on thee is laid;
This the word; I claim it now,
Send me now the promised aid.

High on thy Father's throne,
O look with pity down!
Help, O help! Attend my call,
Captive lead captivity;
King of glory, Lord of all,
Christ, be Lord, be King to me!

I pant to feel thy sway,
And only thee t'obey:
Thee my spirit gasps to meet,
This my one, my ceaseless prayer,
Make, O make my heart thy seat,
O set up thy kingdom there!

Triumph and reign in me,
And spread thy victory;
Hell, and death, and sin control,
Pride, and wrath, and every foe,
All subdue: through all my soul
Conqu'ring and to conquer go!

(*Collection*-1781, #342)

Prayers, Comments & Questions

God our rock, you hear the cries of your people and answer the prayers of the faithful. Grant us the boldness of Hannah that we may persist in prayer, confident in your steadfast love. Amen.

November 22: Christ the King

Preparation for Sunday
Psalm 132:1-18

Thursday
2 Kings 22:1-10
Acts 7:54–8:1a

Friday
2 Kings 22:11-20
1 Corinthians 15:20-28

Saturday
2 Kings 23:1-14
John 3:31-36

Sunday
2 Samuel 23:1-7
Psalm 132:1-18
Revelation 1:4b-8
John 18:33-37

Reflection on Sunday
Psalm 63

Monday
2 Kings 23:15-25
Revelation 11:1-14

Tuesday
1 Samuel 17:55–18:5
Revelation 11:15-19

Wednesday
2 Samuel 2:1-7
John 16:25-33

The General Rule of Discipleship
To witness to Jesus Christ in the world and to follow his teachings
through acts of compassion, justice, worship, and devotion under the guidance of the Holy Spirit.

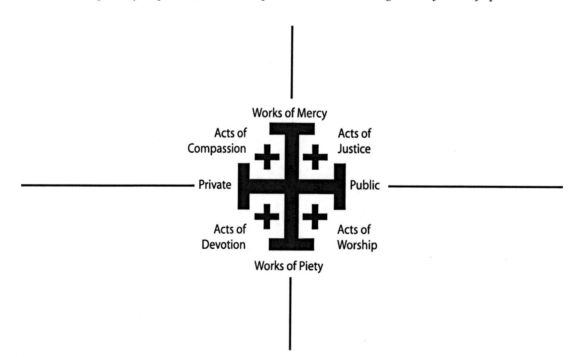

A Word from John Wesley

Above all, stand fast in obedient faith, faith in the God of pardoning mercy, in the God and Father of our Lord Jesus Christ, who hath loved you, and given himself for you. Ascribe to Him all the good you find in yourself; all your peace, and joy, and love; all your power to do and suffer his will, through the Spirit of the living God. Yet, in the mean time, carefully avoid enthusiasm: Impute not the dreams of men to the all-wise God; and expect neither light nor power from him, but in the serious use of all the means he hath ordained.

"Advice to the People Called Methodists"

A Hymn from Charles Wesley

Partners of a glorious hope,
Lift your hearts and voices up.
Jointly let us rise and sing
Christ our Prophet, Priest, and King.
Monuments of Jesu's grace,
Speak we by our lives his praise,
Walk in him we have received,
Show we not in vain believed.

Hence may all our actions flow,
Love the proof that Christ we know;
Mutual love the token be,
Lord, that we belong to thee.
Love, thine image love impart!
Stamp it on our face and heart!
Only love to us be given—
Lord, we ask no other heaven.

(*Collection*-1781, #508:1 & 4)

Prayers, Comments & Questions

Almighty God, you remember the oath you swore to David and so established a glorious realm of salvation through Jesus of Nazareth, his heir. Train our eyes to see your righteous rule, that, standing firmly in hope before the powers of this world, we may heed your voice and be constant in your truth. Amen.

Advent & Christmas

(Year C)

November 29: First Sunday of Advent

Preparation for Sunday
Psalm 25:1-10

Thursday
Nehemiah 9:6-15
1 Thessalonians 5:1-11

Friday
Nehemiah 9:16-25
1 Thessalonians 5:12-22

Saturday
Nehemiah 9:26-31
Luke 21:20-24

Sunday
Jeremiah 33:14-16
Psalm 25:1-10
1 Thessalonians 3:9-13
Luke 21:25-36

Reflection on Sunday
Psalm 90

Monday
Numbers 17:1-11
2 Peter 3:1-18

Tuesday
2 Samuel 7:18-29
Revelation 22:12-16

Wednesday
Isaiah 1:24-31
Luke 11:29-32

The General Rule of Discipleship
*To witness to Jesus Christ in the world and to follow his teachings
through acts of compassion, justice, worship, and devotion under the guidance of the Holy Spirit.*

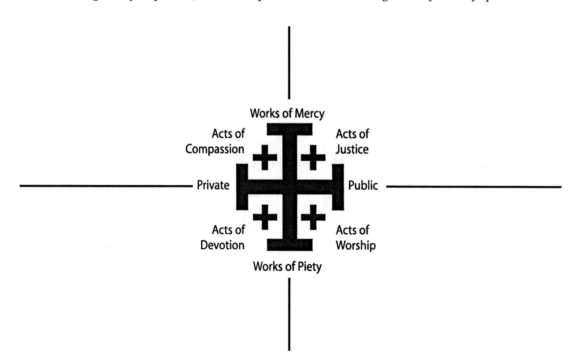

A Word from John Wesley

Be true also to your principles touching opinions and the externals of religion. Use every ordinance which you believe is of God; but beware of narrowness of spirit towards those who use them not. Conform yourself to those modes of worship which you approve; yet love as brethren those who cannot conform. Lay so much stress on opinions, that all your own, if it be possible, may agree with truth and reason; but have a care of anger, dislike, or contempt towards those whose opinions differ from yours.

"Advice to the People Called Methodists"

A Hymn from Charles Wesley

Hearken to the solemn voice,
The awful midnight cry!
Waiting souls, rejoice, rejoice,
And see the bridegroom nigh!
Lo! he comes to keep his word;
Light and joy his looks impart;
Go ye forth to meet your Lord,
And meet him in your heart.

Wait we all in patient hope
Till Christ the Judge shall come;
We shall soon be all caught up
To meet the general doom;
In an hour to us unknown,
As a thief in deepest night,
Christ shall suddenly come down
With all his saints in light.

Happy he whom Christ shall find
Watching to see him come;
Him the Judge of all mankind
Shall bear triumphant home;
Who can answer to his word?
Which of you dares meet his day?
'Rise, and come to Judgment'—Lord,
We rise, and come away.

(*Collection*-1781, #53:1, 4, & 5)

Prayers, Comments & Questions

O God of all the prophets, you herald the coming of the Son of Man by wondrous signs in the heavens and on the earth. Guard our hearts from despair so that we, in the company of the faithful and by the power of your Holy Spirit, may be found ready to raise our heads at the coming near of our redemption, the day of Jesus Christ. Amen.

December 6: Second Sunday of Advent

Preparation for Sunday
Luke 1:68-79

Thursday
Malachi 3:5-12
Philippians 1:12-18a

Friday
Malachi 3:13-18
Philippians 1:18b-26

Saturday
Malachi 4:1-6
Luke 9:1-6

Sunday
Malachi 3:1-4
Luke 1:68-79
Philippians 1:3-11
Luke 3:1-6

Reflection on Sunday
Psalm 126

Monday
Isaiah 40:1-11
Romans 8:22-25

Tuesday
Isaiah 19:18-25
2 Peter 1:2-15

Wednesday
Isaiah 35:3-7
Luke 7:18-30

The General Rule of Discipleship
To witness to Jesus Christ in the world and to follow his teachings
through acts of compassion, justice, worship, and devotion under the guidance of the Holy Spirit.

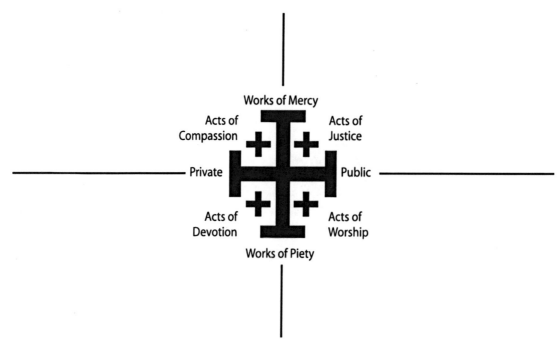

A Word from John Wesley

Glory be to thee, O holy, undivided Trinity, for jointly concurring in the great work of our redemption, and restoring us again to the glorious liberty of the sons of God. Glory be to thee, who, in compassion to human weakness, hast appointed a solemn day for the remembrance of thy inestimable benefits. O let me ever esteem it my privilege and happiness to have a day set apart for the concerns of my soul, a day free from distractions, disengaged from the world, wherein I have nothing to do but to praise and love thee. O let it ever be to me a day sacred to divine love, a day of heavenly rest and refreshment.

"Forms of Prayer for Every Day in the Week"
Sunday Morning

A Hymn from Charles Wesley

He comes! he comes! the Judge severe!
The seventh trumpet speaks him near;
His light'nings flash, his thunders roll;
How welcome to the faithful soul!

From heaven angelic voices sound,
See the almighty Jesus crowned!
Girt with omnipotence and grace,
And glory decks the Saviour's face!

Descending on his azure throne,
He claims the kingdoms for his own;
The kingdoms all obey his word,
And hail him their triumphant Lord!

Shout all the people of the sky,
And all the saints of the Most High;
Our Lord, who now his right obtains,
For ever and for ever reigns.

(*Collection*-1781, #55)

Prayers, Comments & Questions

Out of the embrace of mercy and righteousness, you have brought forth joy and dignity for your people, O Holy One of Israel. Remember now your ancient promise: make straight the paths that lead to you, and smooth the rough ways, that in our day we might bring forth your compassion for all humanity. Amen.

December 13: Third Sunday of Advent

Preparation for Sunday
Isaiah 12:2-6

Thursday
Amos 6:1-8
2 Corinthians 8:1-15

Friday
Amos 8:4-12
2 Corinthians 9:1-15

Saturday
Amos 9:8-15
Luke 1:57-66

Sunday
Zephaniah 3:14-20
Isaiah 12:2-6
Philippians 4:4-7
Luke 3:7-18

Reflection on Sunday
Isaiah 11:1-9

Monday
Numbers 16:1-19
Hebrews 13:7-17

Tuesday
Numbers 16:20-35
Acts 28:23-31

Wednesday
Micah 4:8-13
Luke 7:31-35

The General Rule of Discipleship
*To witness to Jesus Christ in the world and to follow his teachings
through acts of compassion, justice, worship, and devotion under the guidance of the Holy Spirit.*

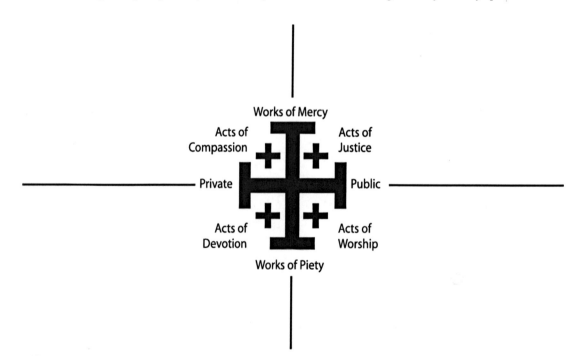

A Word from John Wesley

I confess it is my duty to love thee, my God, with all my heart. Give thy strength unto thy servant, that thy love may fill my heart, and be the motive of all the use I make of my understanding, my affections, my senses, my health, my time, and whatever other talents I have received from thee. Let this, O God, rule my heart without a rival; let it dispose all my thoughts, words, and works; and thus only can I fulfil my duty and thy command, of loving thee "with all my heart, and mind, and soul, and strength."

"Forms of Prayer for Every Day in the Week"
Sunday Morning

A Hymn from Charles Wesley

Ye virgin souls arise,
With all the dead awake.
Unto salvation wise,
Oil in your vessels take:
Upstarting at the midnight cry,
Behold the heavenly bridegroom nigh.

He comes, he comes to call
The nations to his bar,
And raise to glory all
Who fit for glory are;
Made ready for your full reward,
Go forth with joy to meet your Lord.

Then let us wait to hear
The trumpet's welcome sound,
To see our Lord appear,
Watching let us be found;
When Jesus doth the heavens bow,
Be found—as, Lord, thou find'st us now!

(*Collection*-1781, #64:1, 2, & 6)

Prayers, Comments & Questions

O God of the exiles and the lost, you promise restoration and wholeness through the power of Jesus Christ. Give us faith to live joyfully, sustained by your promises as we eagerly await the day when they will be fulfilled for all the world to see, through the coming of your Son, Jesus Christ. Amen.

December 20: Fourth Sunday of Advent

Preparation for Sunday
Psalm 80:1-7

Thursday
Jeremiah 31:31-34
Hebrews 10:10-18

Friday
Isaiah 42:10-18
Hebrews 10:32-39

Saturday
Isaiah 66:7-11
Luke 13:31-35

Sunday
Micah 5:2-5a
Luke 1:46b-55
Hebrews 10:5-10
Luke 1:39-55

Reflection on Sunday
Psalm 113

Monday
Genesis 25:19-28
Colossians 1:15-20

Tuesday
Micah 4:1-5
Ephesians 2:11-22

Wednesday
Micah 4:6-8
2 Peter 1:16-21

The General Rule of Discipleship
To witness to Jesus Christ in the world and to follow his teachings
through acts of compassion, justice, worship, and devotion under the guidance of the Holy Spirit.

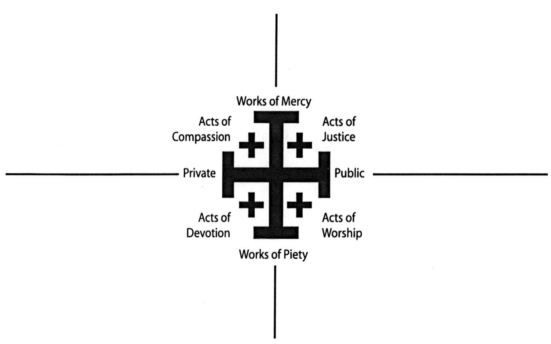

A Word from John Wesley

O thou infinite Goodness, confirm thy past mercies to me, by enabling me, for what remains of my life, to be more faithful than I have hitherto been to this thy great command. For the time I have yet to sojourn upon earth, O let me fulfil this great duty. Permit me not to be in any delusion here; let me not trust in words, or sighs, or tears, but love thee even as thou hast commanded. Let me feel, and then I shall know, what it is to love thee with all my heart.

"Forms of Prayer for Every Day in the Week"
Sunday Morning

A Hymn from Charles Wesley

Father our hearts we lift,
Up to thy gracious throne,
And bless thee for the precious gift,
Of thine incarnate Son:
The gift unspeakable,
We thankfully receive,
And to the world thy goodness tell,
And to thy glory live.

Jesus the holy child,
Doth by his birth declare
That God and man are reconciled,
And one in him we are:
Salvation through his name
To all mankind is given,
And loud his infant cries proclaim,
A peace 'twixt earth and heaven.

(*Hymns for the Nativity of Our Lord*-1745, #9:1 & 2)

Prayers, Comments & Questions

O Shepherd of Israel, you gently support the one who is with child and call forth the Lamb who dances in the womb. Stir our hearts to recognize Christ's coming, as Elizabeth recognized his presence in Mary's radiant obedience to your desire, and open our souls to receive the one who came to love your flock. Amen.

December 27: First Sunday after Christmas

Preparation for Sunday
Luke 1:46b-55

Thursday
Christmas Eve
Micah 6:6-8
Hebrews 10:5-10

Friday
Christmas Day
Isaiah 9:2-7
Psalm 96
Titus 2:11-14
Luke 2:1-20

Saturday
2 Chronicles 24:17-24
Acts 6:1-7; 7:51-60

Sunday
1 Samuel 2:18-20, 26
Psalm 148
Colossians 3:12-17
Luke 2:41-52

Reflection on Sunday
Psalm 147:12-20

Monday
Isaiah 54:1-13
Revelation 21:1-7

Tuesday
1 Chronicles 28:1-10
1 Corinthians 3:10-17

Wednesday
2 Chronicles 1:7-13
Mark 13:32-37

The General Rule of Discipleship
*To witness to Jesus Christ in the world and to follow his teachings
through acts of compassion, justice, worship, and devotion under the guidance of the Holy Spirit.*

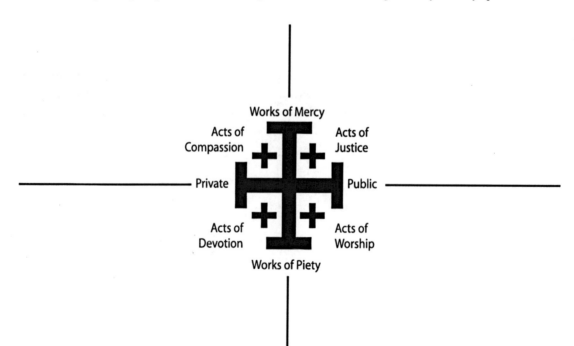

A Word from John Wesley

Deliver me, O God, from too intense an application to even necessary business. I know how this dissipates my thoughts from the one end of all my business, and impairs that lively perception I would ever retain of thee standing at my right hand. I know the narrowness of my heart, and that an eager attention to earthly things leaves it no room for the things of heaven. O teach me to go through all my employments with so truly disengaged a heart, that I may still see thee in all things, and see thee therein as continually looking upon me, and searching my reins; and that I may never impair that liberty of spirit which is necessary for the love of thee.

"Forms of Prayer for Every Day in the Week"

A Hymn from Charles Wesley

Father our hearts we lift,
Up to thy gracious throne,
And bless thee for the precious gift,
Of thine incarnate Son:
The gift unspeakable,
We thankfully receive,
And to the world thy goodness tell,
And to thy glory live.

Jesus the holy child,
Doth by his birth declare
That God and man are reconciled,
And one in him we are:
Salvation through his name
To all mankind is given,
And loud his infant cries proclaim,
A peace 'twixt earth and heaven.

(*Hymns for the Nativity of Our Lord*-1745, #9:1 & 2)

Prayers, Comments & Questions

God of glory, your splendor shines from the manger in Bethlehem, where the Light of the world is humbly born into the darkness of human night. Open our eyes to Christ's presence in the shadows of our world, so that we, like him, may become beacons of your justice, and defenders of all for whom there is no room. Amen.

January 3: Second Sunday after Christmas

Preparation for Sunday
Psalm 147:12-20

Thursday
1 Kings 3:5-14
John 8:12-19

Friday
Holy Name of Jesus
Numbers 6:22-27
Psalm 8
Galatians 4:4-7
Luke 2:15-21

Saturday
Proverbs 1:1-7
James 3:13-18

Sunday
Jeremiah 31:7-14
Psalm 147:12-20
Ephesians 1:3-14
John 1:1-18

The General Rule of Discipleship
To witness to Jesus Christ in the world and to follow his teachings
through acts of compassion, justice, worship, and devotion under the guidance of the Holy Spirit.

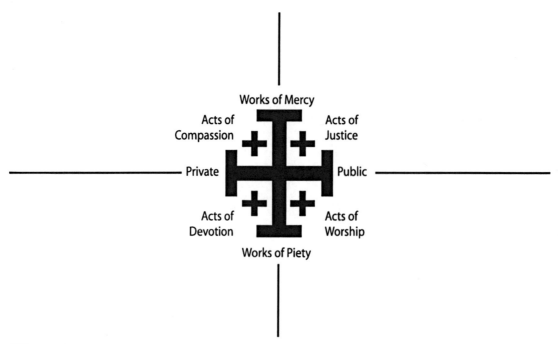

A Word from John Wesley

Above all, deliver me, O my God, from all idolatrous self-love. I know, O God, (blessed be thy infinite mercy for giving me this knowledge,) that this is the root of all evil. I know thou madest me, not to do my own will, but thine. I know, the very corruption of the devil is, the having a will contrary to thine. O be thou my helper against this most dangerous of all idols, that I may both discern all its subtleties, and withstand all its force. O thou who hast commanded me to renounce myself, give me strength, and I will obey thy command. My choice and desire is, to love myself, as all other creatures, in and for thee. O let thy almighty arm so stablish, strengthen, and settle me, that thou mayest ever be the ground and pillar of all my love.

"Forms of Prayer for Every Day in the Week"

A Hymn from Charles Wesley

See the eternal Son of God
A mortal son of man
Dwelling in an earthly clod
Whom heaven cannot contain!
Stand amazed, ye heavens, at this!
See the Lord of earth and skies;
Humbled to the dust he is,
And in a manger lies.

We, earth's children, now rejoice,
The Prince of Peace proclaim;
With heaven's host lift up our voice,
And shout Immanuel's name:
Knees and hearts to him we bow;
Of our flesh and of our bone,
Jesus is our brother now,
And God is all our own.

(*Hymns for the Nativity of Our Lord*-1745, #4:3 & 4)

Prayers, Comments & Questions

God of new beginnings, you wipe away our tears and call us to care for one another. Give us eyes to see your gifts, hearts to embrace all creation, and hands to serve you every day of our lives. We ask this in the name of Jesus. Amen.

Articles

Wesleyan Essentials

Current Reality

The mission and identity of The United Methodist Church in the United States are shaped much more by the culture of market consumerism in which it is immersed than the rich Wesleyan theological tradition from which it emerged. The US church is captive to American culture characterized by individualism, consumerism, and nationalism.

There is hope. The Triune God has power to break the chains that bind us. The God who became one of us in the crucified and risen Jesus Christ has set the church free.

Jesus is calling to The United Methodist Church in the United States and all churches with the same words he proclaimed in Mark 1:15: "The time is fulfilled, and the kingdom of God has come near; repent, and believe the good news." He is beckoning the church to join him in his work of preparing this world for the coming reign of God. He is telling us it is time to turn away from the practices, attitudes, and pride that keep us captive to the dominant culture. He invites us to turn to him, to trust in his grace, and join him in his mission in the world.

We believe The United Methodist Church has within its rich Wesleyan tradition all it needs to claim the liberation Christ offers and to move forward once again as a truly missional movement and church. Our primary theological task is to contextualize the tradition so that it may be taught, internalized, and practiced in a market-driven, postmodern, post-Christian culture.

To that end, we present here the Wesleyan essentials of Christian faith and mission:

Good News: The Sovereign Triune God

- God's Triune name reveals the divine nature is Love. God the Father, Son, and Holy Spirit comprise a community united as one in love. In Trinity God is revealed to be relational. God is not a solitary spirit or being. The Triune God is a matrix of relationship among the three persons of Father, Son, and Spirit. Each person is distinct while sharing intimate relationship with the other two. They interpenetrate one another, participating in one another's life and work. Covenant Love unites and binds the Three as One. In the words of Charles Wesley in his great hymn "Wrestling Jacob," "Thy nature, and thy name is Love."

- The dynamic of love within the Trinity extends toward and into creation. The Father sends the Son as agent of creation and redemption (*logos*, see Genesis 1:1-5 and John 1:1-5). The Father and the Son send the Holy Spirit as the breath that gives life, faith, and hope to the world. The Father, Son, and Holy Spirit create and send the Church as sign and witness of God's reign on earth as it is in heaven. This relational, sending nature reveals God's missional nature.

- Love is incarnate in the Son, Jesus Christ. He is the Prophet who proclaims God's law of love and leads people into holiness. He is God's Priest who forgives, comforts, and heals the brokenness of sin. He is the King of creation who rules with the law of love and justice. Christ's love liberates human beings, communities, and systems from the guilt and power of sin and death, releasing them to participate in his mission of redemption and restoration of the world.

- The Holy Spirit inspires and sustains life in Christ. The Spirit is God at work in the world and in human lives as Advocate, Teacher, and Comforter. The Holy Spirit empowers and equips people to deny themselves, take up their cross daily and follow Jesus (Luke 9:23). Grace is the power of the Holy Spirit that works in the human heart to redeem, heal, and restore the image of Christ damaged and distorted by sin.

- Human beings are created in the image of the Triune God (Genesis 1:26-27). Wesley says in Sermon 141, "Man was what God is, Love." Being created in the image of God is to be created good and for good, with the capacity to love as God loves. This means that human beings are innately relational and social creatures. Individualism is contrary to human character. It contributes to the distortion of human character, communities, and systems. To become fully human requires participation in relationships and communities characterized by mutual interdependence.

Bad News: The Problem of Sin

- Sin is alienation from God. All human beings are damaged by sin (Romans 5:12) because we live in the world that is ruled by powers and principalities opposed to God. None is exempt from the power of sin that shatters the divine image and distorts all human relationships and systems. Wesley writes in Sermon 44 ("Original Sin"), "We have by nature not only no love, but no fear of God." He refers to "inbred sin" because it is the human condition; sin is as natural to us as breathing. It is beyond our power to overcome or control. Apart from God, there is absolutely nothing we can do about it. Inbred sin leads to behavior contrary to love, righteousness, and justice. Sin damages and distorts relationships with God, neighbors, and self.

- Sin distorts and corrupts human relationships and institutions. It permeates every aspect of human life. War, oppression, poverty, disease, hunger, and slavery are symptoms of sin that infect human institutions and endeavors. Sin is insidious. It insinuates itself into all human endeavors, even those whose intentions are good and just.

- Sins (i.e. sinful behaviors and actions) are the transgressing of known laws of God.
  - » "All sin is a transgression of this law, yet it is by no means true, on the other hand, (though we have so often taken it for granted,) that all transgressions of this law are sin: No, not at all; only all voluntary transgressions of it; none else are sins against the Gospel law" (John Wesley, "A Letter to a Member of the Society" CCLIX, May 31, 1771).
- Wesley makes a crucial distinction between actual sins and human faults or mistakes.
  - » "The best of men still need Christ in his priestly office, to atone for their omissions, their short-comings, (as some not improperly speak,) their mistakes in judgment and practice, and their defects of various kinds. For these are all deviations from the perfect law, and consequently need an atonement. Yet that they are not properly sins, we apprehend may appear from the words of St. Paul, 'He that loveth, hath fulfilled the law; for love is the fulfilling of the law' (Romans 13:10). Now, mistakes, and whatever infirmities necessarily flow from the corruptible state of the body, are no way contrary to love; nor therefore, in the Scripture sense, sin." (John Wesley, "A Plain Account of Christian Perfection" §17).

Good News: "For by Grace You Are Saved through Faith"

God's response to sin is redeeming love. God's love is incarnate in the person and work of Jesus of Nazareth who is the Christ. He proclaimed and lived the good news of the reign of God that is breaking into the world now and is coming. Jesus' life, death, and resurrection are a witness to the power and presence of God's reign on earth as it is in heaven. Jesus' reign is revealed in love and justice for all people, especially the poor, vulnerable, and voiceless. His death destroys the powers of sin and death. His resurrection is a declaration of freedom and new life for the world.

Grace is the power and presence of God released into the world by the life, death, and resurrection of Jesus Christ through the power of the Holy Spirit. This grace is freely given and available to all people. God's love is experienced as grace. There is only one grace. People experience grace according to where they stand in relation to Christ. This means that grace is experienced as prevenient, justifying, and sanctifying:

- Prevenient grace awakens us to our condition as sinners who need forgiveness and healing. Grace prepares us to accept God's acceptance in Jesus Christ through repentance. Prevenient grace gives us the ability to turn away from the desolation of sin and toward Christ and life in God's household.
- Justifying grace restores relationship with God and neighbor through faith in Christ
  - » Sins are forgiven.

> » The guilt of sin is removed.
> » Faith is given and accepted as pure gift. Faith is belief *and* trust in God who is love (1 John 4:13-21).
> » Life is aligned with Jesus Christ who is "the way, the truth, and the life" (John 14:6).
> » Justification is God's work for us in the life, death, and resurrection of Jesus Christ.

- Sanctifying grace sustains the life of Christ in us. It is "faith working through love" (Galatians 5:6) so that we may "have the mind of Christ" (Philippians 2:5).

Restored relationship with God (justification) brings new birth (see John 3:3-16). The apostle Paul describes this change when he writes, "So if anyone is in Christ there is a new creation: everything old has passed away; see, everything has become new!" (2 Corinthians 5:17-21).

> » Grace defeats the power of sin to distort and control my life. The power of love replaces the power of sin to govern my thinking and behavior.
> » Grace gives freedom from sin and freedom for love that leads to holiness of heart and life.
> » Holiness of heart and life becomes the new way of life (Matthew 22:34-40; Philippians 2:12-13; Hebrews 12:14).
> » The image of Christ, damaged and distorted by sin, is healed (Philippians 2:5) and the character of Christ is formed in the soul (Galatians 5:22-23).
> » The means of grace (works of piety and works of mercy) become holy habits that form the spiritual gifts for leadership and service in discipleship. The church needs these to participate with Christ in his mission of preparing this world for the coming reign of God.
> » Sanctification is God's work in us by the power of the Holy Spirit, making us like Christ.

The Mission of the Church: To reform the nation and spread scriptural holiness over the land

"'Holy solitaries' is a phrase no more consistent with the gospel than holy adulterers. The gospel of Christ knows of no religion, but social; no holiness but social holiness. 'Faith working by love' is the length and breadth and depth and height of Christian perfection." – John Wesley in the "Preface to Hymns & Sacred Poems"-1739

Christ doesn't call us to live as Christians alone. He calls us into the community of his household, the church. Christ welcomes and brings us home by grace. Like a family, we do not choose who we live and serve with in this community, Christ does (John 15:16). Christ supplies the grace, faith and love sufficient for each person to participate fully in the life of his household. It's up to us to claim the gifts and employ them to serve Christ in the world.

While Christ has saved us by grace through faith, we continue to live in a sinful and broken world. By grace the saved are no longer of the world, but they must live in the world as witnesses to Christ, the good news of the reign of God. We continue to struggle with evil, temptation, and distractions from the life to which Christ calls us. That is why we need the community of support in the household of Christ.

Small groups have historically played a crucial role in the nurture, support, and growth of discipleship in the church. Learning and following the teachings of Jesus Christ is not easy. We need the help and support of fellow Christians, who are our brothers and sisters in holiness of heart and life. Christ calls us to build one another up through mutual support and accountability (Ephesians 4:1-16). "To be together with other Christians in a small group is to open oneself to being formed and transformed in Christ. . . People who do not meet together do not have a pace or place to help one another do the good things of Jesus' ministry. Righteousness flows directly out of community. It is the fruit of face-to-face human encounters where confession and forgiveness are practiced. Justice is the outward product of groups who practice the law of love within their own group context" (Gareth Icenogle, *Biblical Foundations for Small Group Ministry: An Intergenerational Approach*, page 281). Left to ourselves we will turn away from Christ and return to the old life that leads to alienation and death. But when we accept the support and love of fellow sisters and brothers in Christ, we will be more able to resist the temptations of the world and become more dependable disciples.

Small groups have been part of the Church from its beginning. Jesus started his ministry with a small group (Mark 1:16-20; 2:13-17; 3:13-18). The early church was composed of small gatherings of believers who met in homes. Our United Methodist tradition traces its history through the system of small groups developed by John Wesley and the early Methodists.

Wesley was influenced by the Moravians of his time. They were a German pietist sect lead by Count Nikolaus Ludwig von Zinzendorf. He founded an influential Christian community on his estate, Herrnhut, in Moravia. During a visit to Herrnhut in 1738, shortly after his Aldersgate Street experience, John Wesley observed how the Moravian society was divided into small groups known as "bands." These became known as *ecclesiola in ecclesia*, "little churches" within the Church. The purpose of these *ecclesiola* was to provide a place for Christian nurture, teaching, and discipline that was not possible in the larger society or *Ecclesia*.

Upon his return to London, Wesley set about to organize the Fetter Lane society in accord with the Moravian model. "The bands were to number no fewer than five persons and no more than ten, with all members of the society to be so divided. Everyone was to speak 'as freely, plainly and concisely as he [could] the real state of his heart, with his several temptations and deliverances, since the last time of meeting.' Prospective members were to be formed into trial bands, to be 'assisted' for a period of two months before admission, at which point they were admonished to be 'entirely open,' using 'no kind of reserve'" (David Lowes Watson, *The Early Methodist Class Meeting*, page 81). Wesley saw this form of organization for Methodist societies to be a recovery of the model found in

Scripture and practiced in the early, "primitive," church. He saw the *ecclesiola in ecclesia* as enabling the society to become the household of Christ.

However, the Moravian band model did not prove to be as successful as Wesley had hoped. In 1742 Wesley and other Methodist leaders discovered a more suitable small-group model that became a hallmark of the Methodist movement. The Class Meeting emerged out of the need to retire a debt Wesley had incurred for the building of the first Methodist meeting house, called the "New Room," in Bristol. The members of the Methodist societies contributed a penny a week until the debt was retired. To collect the money the societies were divided into groups of twelve according to neighborhood. These groups were called "classes." Leaders were assigned to the classes. Each week the leaders visited the homes of each member in his or her class to collect a penny. If, for any reason, the member was not able to contribute a penny the leader would contribute for them. At the end of the month the leaders met with Wesley to turn in the collected money and to inform him about the state of members in the respective classes. Because weekly visits to each home became too time consuming, it was agreed that the classes would assemble each week with the respective leaders. Wesley soon realized the pastoral role of these meetings, and the Methodist class meeting was born. It soon formed the sinews of the Methodist evangelical revival and movement (Watson, 93–94).

From 1742 to near the end of the nineteenth century every Methodist was required to be part of a class. The Methodists gathered once a week to pray, read and study the Bible, sing hymns, share fellowship, and give an account of their discipleship. They were bound together, like family, in their common love for Christ and one another and their desire to grow in holiness of heart and life. Together, they encouraged one another in practicing the means of grace, doing good, and sharing their faith that brought thousands of people to Christ and lifted themselves and many others out of poverty.

Alongside the classes were the bands and select societies that formed a distinctively Methodist system of Christian formation. While every Methodist was expected to participate in a class, the bands and select societies were voluntary groups. Membership in the classes was determined by where people lived. They were mixed groups of men and women, married and single, under the leadership of a mature Christian man or woman selected by Wesley or one of his preachers. Bands were for those who had experienced the assurance of forgiveness of their sins and were ready for a deeper level of sharing and accountability. They were smaller in size and segregated according to gender and marital status. Leadership in the bands was shared. They were characterized by mutual accountability and support for holiness.

Finally, the select societies were for those determined to go onto perfection in love. "To be specific, it was created for those who were actively pressing after the experience of entire sanctification, to provide more serious mutual support and accountability for their quest. This need for accountability was even greater for those who claimed the experience, since it was open to continuing growth and (experience proved) capable of being lost" (Randy Maddox, *Responsible Grace: John Wesley's Practical Theology*, page 213). This system of small groups with progressive levels of support, accountability, and intimacy emerged from Wesley's theology and his understanding of the way of salvation.

Inherent in this Wesleyan system of Christian formation is the importance of personal relationship with God and with those with whom God gives us to live in the household of Christ. The means of grace were given by God to help build and sustain those relationships. In this sense the Methodist societies functioned much like a family system. People were welcomed and treated as sisters and brothers related to one another through their common relationship with God in Jesus Christ. The means of grace were the practices and rituals all shared in common. They facilitated the flow of grace throughout the societies, classes, bands, and select societies.

The Methodists "watched over one another in love," giving support and encouragement for growth in faith, hope, and love. The system of classes, bands, and select societies provided a means of progressive catechesis, support, and accountability people needed as their faith matured. Wesley believed and taught that salvation was progressive. It was a process of growth and maturation. The system he developed to help people experience "grace upon grace" (John 1:16) and grow in their love for God and neighbor and their obedience to Christ reflects his convictions and experience of human need and the work of grace in the world.

The Lord's Supper Makes Disciples in the Church

The Lord's Supper is a means of grace. Wesley believed that, next to prayer, it is the grandest, most efficacious and powerful of all the spiritual disciplines. This is why Charles writes in his great Eucharistic hymn "O the Depth of Love Divine," "Sure and real is the grace." He is saying here that we can go to the Lord's table with confidence knowing that Christ will meet us there. His forgiveness and healing love are a sure thing. They are a sure thing because God is trustworthy and true. When we come to the table with open hearts and empty hands we can expect to meet the risen Christ.

Grace is real. We can see, touch, smell, and taste it when we eat the bread and drink the wine at Christ's table. We can know grace is real because we do not come to the table to eat and drink alone. We are members of Christ's body, the Church that is "one with Christ, one with *each* other, and one in ministry to all the world."[1] Grace flows through the relationships God gives to us in the congregation. We learn how to give and receive love through relationships with those whom God gives to us. For Wesley, grace is not merely an idea or concept or thing. For Wesley, grace is a person. Grace does not come to us as "something." Grace comes to us as "someone." And that someone is named Jesus Christ.

---

1. This line is taken from the *epiclesis* near the end of the Great Thanksgiving found on page 10 in *The United Methodist Hymnal*. The *epiclesis* is the invocation of the Holy Spirit to make the bread and wine on the table to become for us the body and blood of Christ "that we may be for the world the body of Christ, redeemed by his blood." This is the point in the prayer when the bread and wine are consecrated and ready to be shared with the congregation.

The Lord's Supper is a means of grace that "perfects us." This means that it is a practice through which we become fully the persons God created us to be, in Christ. The sacrament is the reliable place where we know God will meet us and give himself to us in the form of bread and wine. The food God gives at his table supplies the grace we need to be his witnesses in the world through works of mercy (acts of compassion and justice). As we feed on this grace it opens our hearts to the power of the Holy Spirit to root out the remnants of inbred (original) sin and to heal the sin-distorted image of Christ. Regular and frequent participation in the sacrament, joined with faith, hope, and love, removes the blockages to grace. As the blockages come down, grace fills us up with the love of God. As we participate in, and cooperate with, the healing power of the Holy Spirit, God fills us up to overflowing with pure love.

Filled with God's love, Christ sends us from his table into the world to serve with him. At the table he feeds us the food we need to participate in his mission of preparing this world for the coming reign of God. In the bread and wine Christ gives himself to us so we can be his representatives in the world (2 Corinthians 5:20–6:2).

The Lord's Supper is a reliable means of grace in which God promises to meet us at his table. Our part is to show up, receive the gifts he gives, and serve with him in the world he loves. The rest is mystery. "It is a divinely chosen way, which creates communion between God and the church; hence we are to observe it. We ask to taste the heavenly powers of the sacramental bread and wine, not to understand them. God's gift is to bless us. Our response is not to ask questions but to bow in wonder and adoration."[2] Understanding how God conveys grace through bread and wine is less important than simply showing up with open hearts and empty hands to receive the free gift of God's life and love.

Conclusion

The Wesleyan tradition is an expression of incarnational Christianity. It teaches that "the soul and the body make a *human*. The Spirit and discipline make a Christian." Charles Wesley expresses this incarnational faith in one of his hymns:

> Plead we thus for faith alone,
> Faith which by our works is shown;
> God it is who justifies,
> Only faith the grace applies,
> Active faith that lives within,
> Conquers earth, and hell, and sin,
> Sanctifies, and makes us whole,
> Forms the Saviour in the soul.

---

2. Laurence Hull Stookey, *Eucharist: Christ's Feast with the Church* (Nashville, TN: Abingdon Press, 1993), 168.

Let us for this faith contend,
Sure salvation is its end;
Heaven already is begun,
Everlasting life is won.
Only let us persevere
Till we see our Lord appear;
Never from the rock remove,
Saved by faith which works by love.

Discipleship is the way of life, shaped by obedience to the teachings of Jesus. It involves the whole person: heart, head, and hands. There is no part of human life or experience that is excluded from Christ and his claim on our life. This means that salvation means much more than being assured a place in heaven after you die. Rather, the Wesleyan tradition teaches that "heaven already is begun" here and now. Our life with Christ is both a future promise and present reality. Those who are saved by grace through faith (Ephesians 2:8) must witness to Jesus Christ in the world and follow his teachings through acts of compassion, justice, worship, and devotion under the guidance of the Holy Spirit. Their new life is shaped by the cross-shaped life described by Jesus when he summarized his teachings in Matthew 22:37-40:

He said to him, "'You shall love the Lord your God with all your heart, and with all your soul, and with all your mind.' This is the greatest and first commandment. And the second is like it: 'You shall love your neighbor as yourself.' On these two commandments hang all the law and the prophets."

When Christians embrace and practice Jesus' discipline of love, the Savior is formed in the soul. Christians then become his workforce in the mission of redeeming this world and preparing it for the coming reign of God.

Congregations that embrace Jesus' culture of mission-shaped discipleship become outposts of the kingdom of God. They understand that they are not the kingdom, but that they represent God's reign in the midst of the world. When people visit their worship services, participate in their programs, or step foot onto the property they immediately recognize in whose name the congregation exists and serves. They see that the church is more than a gathering of like-minded pious people. They see that the church is a community that exists to serve with Christ in the world that he loves.

For in Christ, neither our most conscientious religion nor disregard of religion amount to anything. What matters is something far more interior: faith expressed in love. (Galatians 5:6, *The Message*)

The Nature, Design, and General Rules of Our United Societies

In the latter end of the year 1739, eight or ten persons came to Mr. Wesley in London, who appeared to be deeply convinced of sin, and earnestly groaning for redemption. They desired, as did two or three more the next day, that he would spend some time with them in prayer, and advise them how to flee from the wrath to come, which they saw continually hanging over their heads. That he might have more time for this great work, he appointed a day when they might all come together, which from thenceforward they did every week, namely, on Thursday in the evening. To these, and as many more as desired to join with them (for their number increased daily), he gave those advices from time to time which he judged most needful for them, and they always concluded their meeting with prayer suited to their several necessities.

This was the rise of the **United Society**, first in Europe, and then in America. Such a society is no other than "a company of men having the *form* and seeking the *power* of godliness, united in order to pray together, to receive the word of exhortation, and to watch over one another in love, that they may help each other to work out their salvation."

That it may the more easily be discerned whether they are indeed working out their own salvation, each society is divided into smaller companies, called **classes**, according to their respective places of abode. There are about twelve persons in a class, one of whom is styled the **leader**. It is his duty:

1. To see each person in his class once a week at least, in order:

   - to inquire how their souls prosper;
   - to advise, reprove, comfort or exhort, as occasion may require;
   - to receive what they are willing to give toward the relief of the preachers, church, and poor.

2. To meet the ministers and the stewards of the society once a week, in order:

   - to inform the minister of any that are sick, or of any that walk disorderly and will not be reproved;
   - to pay the stewards what they have received of their several classes in the week preceding.

There is only one condition previously required of those who desire admission into these societies: "a desire to flee from the wrath to come, and to be saved from their sins." But wherever this is really fixed in the soul it will be shown by its fruits.

It is therefore expected of all who continue therein that they should continue to evidence their desire of salvation,

First: By doing no harm, by avoiding evil of every kind, especially that which is most generally practiced, such as:

- The taking of the name of God in vain.
- The profaning the day of the Lord, either by doing ordinary work therein or by buying or selling.
- Drunkenness: buying or selling spirituous liquors, or drinking them, unless in cases of extreme necessity.
- Slaveholding; buying or selling slaves.
- Fighting, quarreling, brawling, brother going to law with brother; returning evil for evil, or railing for railing; the using many words in buying or selling.
- The buying or selling goods that have not paid the duty.
- The giving or taking things on usury—i.e., unlawful interest.
- Uncharitable or unprofitable conversation; particularly speaking evil of magistrates or of ministers.
- Doing to others as we would not they should do unto us.
- Doing what we know is not for the glory of God, as:
  - » The putting on of gold and costly apparel.
  - » The taking such diversions as cannot be used in the name of the Lord Jesus.
  - » The singing those songs, or reading those books, which do not tend to the knowledge or love of God.
  - » Softness and needless self-indulgence.
  - » Laying up treasure upon earth.
  - » Borrowing without a probability of paying; or taking up goods without a probability of paying for them.

It is expected of all who continue in these societies that they should continue to evidence their desire of salvation,

Secondly: By doing good; by being in every kind merciful after their power; as they have opportunity, doing good of every possible sort, and, as far as possible, to all men:

To their bodies, of the ability which God giveth, by giving food to the hungry, by clothing the naked, by visiting or helping them that are sick or in prison.

To their souls, by instructing, reproving, or exhorting all we have any intercourse with; trampling under foot that enthusiastic doctrine that "we are not to do good unless our hearts be free to it."

By doing good, especially to them that are of the household of faith or groaning so to be; employing them preferably to others; buying one of another, helping each other in business, and so much the more because the world will love its own and them only.

By all possible diligence and frugality, that the gospel be not blamed.

By running with patience the race which is set before them, denying themselves, and taking up their cross daily; submitting to bear the reproach of Christ, to be as the filth and offscouring of the world; and looking that men should say all manner of evil of them falsely, for the Lord's sake.

It is expected of all who desire to continue in these societies that they should continue to evidence their desire of salvation,

Thirdly: By attending upon all the ordinances of God; such are:

- The public worship of God.
- The ministry of the Word, either read or expounded.
- The Supper of the Lord.
- Family and private prayer.
- Searching the Scriptures.
- Fasting or abstinence.

These are the General Rules of our societies; all of which we are taught of God to observe, even in his written Word, which is the only rule, and the sufficient rule, both of our faith and practice. And all these we know his Spirit writes on truly awakened hearts. If there be any among us who observe them not, who habitually break any of them, let it be known unto them who watch over that soul as they who must give an account. We will admonish him of the error of his ways. We will bear with him for a season. But then, if he repent not, he hath no more place among us. We have delivered our own souls.

The General Rule of Discipleship

The General Rule of Discipleship is a contemporary restatement of the General Rules. It distills the General Rules down to a single, straightforward statement that can be easily memorized:

**To witness to Jesus Christ in the world and to
follow his teachings through acts of
compassion, justice, worship, and devotion
under the guidance of the Holy Spirit.**

The General Rule of Discipleship is a succinct description of discipleship. It begins by acknowledging that a disciple is one who is a witness to Jesus Christ. This tells us that he or she knows Jesus and can tell others who he is and what he is doing in the world.

Secondly, a disciple lives and witnesses in the world. This acknowledges that disciples, and the church, are with Christ in the world. Discipleship is not about the enjoyment of personal blessings. It is much more about walking and serving with Christ in the world. When Christ calls us to follow him, he calls us to follow him into the world which he loves.

Thirdly, a disciple follows Jesus by obeying his teachings. The General Rule tells us that discipleship is a relationship with Christ. Like any significant relationship, disciples participate in practices that draw them to Christ and keep them with him. Jesus said in Luke 9:23, "If any want to become my followers, let them deny themselves and take up their cross daily and follow me." Self-denial is putting the needs and interests of the beloved ahead of your own. In the context of discipleship the grace of Christ enables you to make Christ's interests your own. The cross disciples must take up each day is obedience to Jesus' teachings summarized in Mark 12:30-31: "You shall love the Lord your God with all your heart, and with all your soul, and with all your mind, and with all your strength. . . You shall love your neighbor as yourself." Disciples grow in loving God (the cross's vertical axis) through practicing acts of worship and devotion. Disciples grow in loving God by loving those whom God loves, as God loves them through acts of compassion and justice (the cross's horizontal axis). As disciples take up the cross of obedience to Jesus' commands they open themselves to grace and grow in holiness of heart and life.

Finally, the General Rule of Discipleship tells us that witnessing to Jesus Christ in the world and following his teachings are guided by the Holy Spirit. This tells us that disciples cannot follow Jesus alone, by their own strength. Only the Holy Spirit, working in them by grace, makes discipleship and subsequent growth in holiness of heart and life possible.

The General Rule of Discipleship helps disciples to maintain balance among all the teachings of Jesus. This balance is represented by the Jerusalem cross (below). The support and accountability provided by a Covenant Discipleship group helps disciples to walk with Christ in the world by practicing both works of mercy (loving the neighbor) and works of piety (loving God). It also helps to maintain balance between the personal and public dimensions of discipleship.

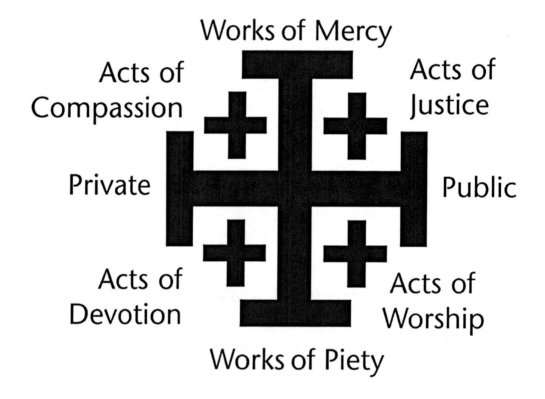

Covenant Discipleship Groups

Covenant

Covenant is God's word for "relationship." Covenant is God's way of **love**. Covenant tells us that God seeks and keeps relationships with others. The nature of God's covenant is self-giving love. Jesus Christ is God's covenant love in flesh and blood. We experience this love as **grace**; responsible grace. It is God's hand, open and outstretched to the world.

Christians are people who accept God's offer of covenant love in the water of baptism. They respond by turning away from sin and accepting the freedom and power God gives to resist evil. They confess Jesus Christ as Savior, put all their trust in his grace, and promise to serve him as Lord within the community of the church. Christians understand that the life of covenant love cannot be lived alone; it requires a community of prayer, forgiveness, and love.

Christians are covenant people.

Discipleship

Discipleship is how Christians live out their covenant with God. It is the way of life shaped by the teachings of Jesus Christ, summarized by him in Mark 12:30-31:

> You shall love the Lord your God with all your heart, and with all your
> soul, and with all your mind, and with all your strength. . . . you shall love
> your neighbor as yourself.

A *disciple* is a person striving to conform his or her life to the life of a beloved teacher. A disciple seeks to become *like* the teacher. Disciples of Jesus Christ are Christians who align their own desires, goals, and habits with the desires, goals, and habits of Jesus Christ.

The apostle Paul describes the goal of discipleship in Philippians 2:5: "Let the same mind be in you that was in Christ Jesus."

Groups

Groups are discipleship incubators. It takes a community of love and forgiveness to make disciples.

Jesus gave his disciples a new commandment:

> ". . . (L)ove one another. Just as I have loved you, you also should love one another. By this everyone will know that you are my disciples, if you have love for one another." (John 13:34-35)

Disciples obey this new commandment when they meet regularly in small groups. They pray for one another, the church and the world. They also give an account of how they have walked with Jesus in the world since they last met. The group works together to help one another become more dependable and mature disciples of Jesus Christ and leaders in discipleship for the church's mission in the world.

Wesleyan Disciple-making

Small groups that focus on mutual accountability and support for discipleship are the "method" of Methodism. These groups have their roots firmly planted in the Wesleyan tradition. The roots go even deeper when you consider that John Wesley described Methodism as his attempt to re-tradition "primitive" Christianity. He said:

> A Methodist is one who has "the love of God shed abroad in his heart by the Holy Ghost given unto him (or her)." —from "The Character of a Methodist"

Covenant Discipleship groups are a way of helping Christians to grow in loving God with all their heart, soul, mind, and strength and loving their neighbor as themselves. They are a proven and effective way of forming **leaders in discipleship** who in turn disciple others and help the congregation to live out its mission with Christ in the world.

Covenant Discipleship groups form Christ-centered people who lead Christ-centered congregations that participate in Christ's ongoing work of preparing the world for the coming reign of God, on earth as it is in heaven. (Matthew 6:10; Luke 11:2)

The General Rule of Discipleship

The General Rule of Discipleship helps Covenant Discipleship group members to practice a balanced and varied discipleship. The General Rule is a contemporary re-statement of The General Rules John Wesley developed for the Methodist societies in 1742. It is simple and elegant:

To witness to Jesus Christ in the world and to follow his teachings through acts of compassion, justice, worship, and devotion under the guidance of the Holy Spirit.

Covenant Discipleship groups write a covenant that spells out how they will follow the teachings of Jesus Christ in their daily lives, shaped by the General Rule. The group's covenant serves as the agenda for the weekly one-hour meeting.

Covenant Discipleship Groups Are . . .

- up to seven persons who meet for one hour each week
- guided by a covenant they write, shaped by the General Rule of Discipleship
- where Christians give a weekly account of how they have witnessed to Jesus Christ in the world and followed his teachings, guided by the group's covenant
- where Christians help one another become more dependable disciples of Jesus Christ
- a proven and effective way of nurturing and identifying leaders in discipleship the church needs to live out its mission with Christ in the world

Put the names of your Covenant Discipleship Group members here.

To Learn More

visit http://www.gbod.org/covenantdiscipleship

Contact: Director of Wesleyan Leadership
GBOD
PO Box 340003
Nashville, TN 37203 0003
Email: cdgroups@gbod.org
Telephone: (877)899-2780, ext. 1765 (toll free)

Recommended Resources

Accountable Discipleship: Living in God's Household by Steven W. Manskar
Provides biblical, theological, and historic foundations for Covenant Discipleship

Covenant Discipleship: Christian Formation through Mutual Accountability by David Lowes Watson
Essential resource for congregational leaders and Covenant Discipleship group members; provides valuable information on how to form groups, how to write a covenant, and how to lead a meeting

Forming Christian Disciples: The Role of Covenant Discipleship and Class Leaders in the Congregation by David Lowes Watson
Written for congregational leaders to help them understand where Covenant Disciples fit in the missional life of a congregation; provides a proven and effective step-by-step process for introducing Covenant Discipleship to a congregation

Class Leaders: Recovering a Tradition by David Lowes Watson
Introduces congregational leaders and Covenant Discipleship group members to the historic practice of Methodist lay pastoral leadership that the church of today needs

A Disciple's Journal by Steven W. Manskar
Designed for use by Covenant Discipleship group members; it helps users read their Bible and pray every day; provides space to record acts of compassion, justice, worship, and devotion each week; the book is based on the Revised Common Lectionary and is published annually to coincide with the church's liturgical calendar

The Wesleyan Way of Making Disciples

Help us to help each other, Lord,
Each other's cross to bear;
Let each his friendly aid afford,
And feel his brother's care.

Help us to build each other up,
Our little stock improve;
Increase our faith, confirm our hope,
And perfect us in love.

In a Christian believer **love** sits upon the throne, which is erected in the inmost soul; namely, love of God and [all people], which fills the whole heart, and reigns without a rival. In a circle near the throne are all **holy tempers**: long-suffering, gentleness, meekness, goodness, fidelity, temperance— and if any other is comprised in 'the mind which was in Christ Jesus'. In an exterior circle are all the **works of mercy**, whether to the souls or bodies of [all people]. By these we exercise all holy tempers; by these we continually improve them, so that all these are real means of grace, although this is not commonly adverted to. Next to these are those that are usually termed **works of piety**: reading and hearing the Word, public, family, private prayer, receiving the Lord's Supper, fasting or abstinence. Lastly, that his followers may the more effectually provoke one another to love, holy tempers, and good works, our blessed Lord has united them together in one—**the church**, dispersed all over the earth; a little emblem of which, of the church universal, we have in every particular Christian congregation.

(John Wesley from Sermon 92: "On Zeal," § II.5)

Excerpts from Sermon 85:
On Working Out Your Salvation

John Wesley, 1785

> Therefore, my beloved, just as you have always obeyed me, not only in my presence, but much more now in my absence, work out your own salvation with fear and trembling; for it is God who is at work in you, enabling you both to will and to work for his good pleasure. (Philippians 2:12-13)

If ever you desire that God should work in you that faith whereof cometh both present and eternal salvation, by the grace already given, fly from all sin as from the face of a serpent; carefully avoid every evil word and work; yea, abstain from all appearance of evil. And 'learn to do well'; be zealous of good works, of works of piety, as well as works of mercy. Use family prayer, and cry to God in secret. Fast in secret, and 'your Father which seeth in secret, he will reward you openly.' 'Search the Scriptures'; hear them in public, read them in private, and meditate therein. At every opportunity be a partaker of the Lord's Supper. 'Do this in remembrance of him,' and he will meet you at his own table. Let your conversation be with the children of God, and see that it 'be in grace, seasoned with salt'. As ye have time, do good unto all men, to their souls and to their bodies. And herein 'be ye steadfast, unmovable, always abounding in the work of the Lord.' It then only remains that ye deny yourselves and take up your cross daily. Deny yourselves every pleasure which does not prepare you for taking pleasure in God, and willingly embrace every means of drawing near to God, though it be a cross, though it be grievous to flesh and blood. Thus when you have redemption in the blood of Christ, you will 'go on to perfection'; till, 'walking in the light, as he is in the light', you are enabled to testify that 'he is faithful and just', not only 'to forgive your sins', but 'to cleanse you from all unrighteousness.' . . .

First, God worketh in you; therefore you can work. . . .

Therefore inasmuch as God works in you, you are now able to work out your own salvation. Since he worketh in you of his own good pleasure, without any merit of yours, both to will and to do, it is possible for you to fulfil all righteousness. . . .

Secondly, God worketh in you; therefore you must work: you must be 'workers together with him'; otherwise he will cease working. . . .

'(H)e that made us without ourselves, will not save us without ourselves.'

Plead we thus for faith alone,
Faith which by our works is shown;
God it is who justifies,
Only faith the grace applies,
Active faith that lives within,
Conquers earth, and hell, and sin,
Sanctifies, and makes us whole,
Forms the Saviour in the soul.

CHARLES WESLEY

Notes

Notes

Notes

Notes

CPSIA information can be obtained at www.ICGtesting.com
Printed in the USA
BVOW06s1546181114

375529BV00002B/3/P